God's Encouraging Word

Compiled by
Clarence L. Blasier

**All Scripture is from
The King James Version of the Bible**

D0180607

THEE OUTLET

A BARBOUR BOOK

ISBN 1-55748-295-0

Published by   Barbour and Company, Inc.
                 P.O. Box 719
                 Uhrichsville, Oh 44683

Printed in the United States of America

PREFACE

So shall my word be that goeth forth out of my mouth: it shall not return unto me void, but it shall accomplish that which I please, and it shall prosper in the thing whereto I sent it.
Isaiah 55:11

What a wonderful blessing it is to be able to trust in God's Living Word for guidance, for comfort, for correction, for instruction in righteousness, for victory in daily living, for the *"pulling down of strong holds,"* and for encouragement in every aspect of our lives! His Word is the *"Sword of the Spirit"* and will not return to Him empty.

The Scriptures contained in this book have been carefully chosen with your victories and concerns in mind. There are no editorial comments, only encouraging Scripture that will most minister to your needs. You will find each selection to be easily understood regardless of your degree of spiritual maturity or your Bible version preference.

- continue -

This is not a book meant to be read quickly from cover to cover. Your greatest blessings will come from prayerfully meditating on each passage of Scripture. Many will have immediate application as God speaks to your individual need at a particular time. These you may want to identify by writing your comment in the margin, or you may even commit to memory those passages with special meaning for you.

You may also want to read many of the selections in their original context. Oftentimes, that which precedes or follows will strengthen your trust in how our great God can and will provide His grace and encouragement to you.

May the Lord richly bless you as He speaks to you through "GOD'S ENCOURAGING WORD."

Clarence L. Blasier

God's
Encouraging
Word

THOU WILT keep him in perfect peace, whose mind is stayed on thee: because he trusteth in thee.

Trust ye in the Lord for ever: for in the Lord JEHOVAH is everlasting strength.

Isaiah 26:3,4

BEHOLD, the eye of the Lord is upon them that fear him, upon them that hope in his mercy;

To deliver their soul from death, and to keep them alive in famine.

Our soul waiteth for the Lord: he is our help and our shield.

For our heart shall rejoice in him, because we have trusted in his holy name.

Let thy mercy, O Lord, be upon us, according as we hope in thee.

Psalm 33:18-22

WHO SHALL SEPARATE us from the love of Christ? shall tribulation, or distress, or persecution, or famine, or nakedness, or peril, or sword?

As it is written, For thy sake we are killed all the day long; we are accounted as sheep for the slaughter.

Nay, in all these things we are more than conquerors through him that loved us.

For I am persuaded, that neither death, nor life, nor angels, nor principalities, nor powers, nor things present, nor things to come,

Nor height, nor depth, nor any other creature, shall be able to separate us from the love of God, which is in Christ Jesus our Lord.

Romans 8:35-39

BLESSED IS THE MAN whose strength is in thee; in whose heart are the ways of them.

Who passing through the valley of Baca make it a well; the rain also filleth the pools.

They go from strength to strength, every one of them in Zion appeareth before God.

Psalm 84:5-7

FOR THIS CAUSE I bow my knees unto the Father of our Lord Jesus Christ,

Of whom the whole family in heaven and earth is named,

That he would grant you, according to the riches of his glory, to be strengthened with might by his Spirit in the inner man;

That Christ may dwell in your hearts by faith; that ye, being rooted and grounded in love,

May be able to comprehend with all saints what is the breadth, and length, and depth, and height;

And to know the love of Christ, which passeth knowledge, that ye might be filled with all the fulness of God.

Ephesians 3:14-19

I WILL PRAISE THEE, O Lord my God, with all my heart: and I will glorify thy name for evermore.

For great is thy mercy toward me: and thou hast delivered my soul from the lowest hell.

Psalm 86:12,13

BUT AS IT IS WRITTEN, Eye hath not seen, nor ear heard, neither have entered into the heart of man, the things which God hath prepared for them that love him.

I Corinthians 2:9

HE THAT DWELLETH in the secret place of the most High shall abide under the shadow of the Almighty.

I will say of the Lord, He is my refuge and my fortress: my God; in him will I trust.

Surely he shall deliver thee from the snare of the fowler, and from the noisome pestilence.

He shall cover thee with his feathers, and under his wings shalt thou trust: his truth shall be thy shield and buckler.

Thou shalt not be afraid for the terror by night; nor for the arrow that flieth by day;

Nor for the pestilence that walketh in darkness; nor for the destruction that wasteth at noonday.

A thousand shall fall at thy side, and ten thousand at thy right hand; but it shall not come nigh thee.

Only with thine eyes shalt thou behold and see the reward of the wicked.

Because thou has made the Lord, which is my refuge, even the most High, thy habitation;

There shall no evil befall thee, neither shall any plague come nigh thy dwelling.

For he shall give his angels charge over thee, to keep thee in all thy ways.

They shall bear thee up in their hands, lest thou dash thy foot against a stone.

Thou shalt tread upon the lion and adder: the young lion and the dragon shalt thou trample under feet.

Because he hath set his love upon me, therefore will I deliver him: I will set him on high, because he hath known my name.

He shall call upon me, and I will answer him: I will be with him in trouble; I will deliver him, and honour him.

With long life will I satisfy him, and shew him my salvation.

Psalm 91

TRUST IN THE LORD with all thine heart; and lean not unto thine own understanding.

In all thy ways acknowledge him, and he shall direct thy paths.

Proverbs 3:5,6

IF THOU, LORD, shouldest mark iniquities, O Lord, who shall stand?

But there is forgiveness with thee, that thou mayest be feared.

I wait for the Lord, my soul doth wait, and in his word do I hope.

My soul waiteth for the Lord more than they that watch for the morning: I say, more than they that watch for the morning.

Psalm 130:3-6

AND IT CAME TO PASS, that at even the quails came up, and covered the camp: and in the morning the dew lay round about the host.

And when the dew that lay was gone up, behold, upon the face of the wilderness there lay a small round thing, as small as the hoar frost on the ground.

And when the children of Israel saw it, they said one to another, It is manna: for they wist not what it was. And Moses said unto them, This is the bread which the Lord hath given you to eat.

Exodus 16:13-15

THOUGH I WALK in the midst of trouble, thou wilt revive me: thou shalt stretch forth thine hand against the wrath of mine enemies, and thy right hand shall save me.

The Lord will perfect that which concerneth me: thy mercy, O Lord, endureth for ever: forsake not the works of thine own hands.

Psalm 138:7,8

JESUS CHRIST the same yesterday, and to day and for ever.

Hebrews 13:8

OFFER UNTO GOD thanksgiving; and pay thy vows unto the most High:

And call upon me in the day of trouble: I will deliver thee, and thou shalt glorify me.

Psalm 50:14,15

FOR GOD so loved the world, that he gave his only begotten Son, that whosoever believeth in him should not perish, but have everlasting life.

John 3:16

BLESSED ARE the poor in spirit: for theirs is the kingdom of heaven.

Blessed are they that mourn: for they shall be comforted.

Blessed are the meek: for they shall inherit the earth.

Blessed are they which do hunger and thirst after righteousness: for they shall be filled.

Blessed are the merciful: for they shall obtain mercy.

Blessed are the pure in heart: for they shall see God.

Blessed are the peacemakers: for they shall be called the children of God.

Blessed are they which are persecuted for righeousness' sake: for theirs is the kingdom of heaven.

Blessed are ye, when men shall revile you, and persecute you, and shall say all manner of evil against you falsely, for my sake.

Rejoice, and be exceeding glad: for great is your reward in heaven: for so persecuted they the prophets which were before you.

Matthew 5:3-12

FOR THOU art my hope, O Lord God: thou art my trust from my youth.

By thee have I been holden up from the womb: thou art he that took me out of my mother's bowels: my praise shall be continually of thee.

I am as a wonder unto many; but thou art my strong refuge.

Psalm 71:5-7

THEN HE ANSWERED and spake unto me, saying, This is the word of the Lord unto Zerubbabel, saying, Not by might, nor by power, but by my spirit, saith the Lord of hosts.

Zechariah 4:6

COME NOW, and let us reason together, saith the Lord: though your sins be as scarlet, they shall be as white as snow; though they be red like crimson, they shall be as wool.

If ye be willing and obedient, ye shall eat the good of the land:

But if ye refuse and rebel, ye shall be devoured with the sword: for the mouth of the Lord hath spoken it.

Isaiah 1:18-20

AND WHEN he had spoken these things, while they beheld, he was taken up; and a cloud received him out of their sight.

And while they looked stedfastly toward heaven as he went up, behold, two men stood by them in white apparel;

Which also said, Ye men of Galilee, why stand ye gazing up into heaven? this same Jesus, which is taken up from you into heaven, shall so come in like manner as ye have seen him go into heaven.

Acts 1:9-11

THE LORD is my shepherd; I shall not want.

He maketh me to lie down in green pastures: he leadeth me beside the still waters.

He restoreth my soul: he leadeth me in the paths of righteousness for his name's sake.

Yea, though I walk through the valley of the shadow of death, I will fear no evil: for thou art with me; thy rod and thy staff they comfort me.

Thou preparest a table before me in the presence of mine enemies: thou anointest my head with oil; my cup runneth over.

Surely goodness and mercy shall follow me all the days of my life: and I will dwell in the house of the Lord for ever.

Psalm 23

BUT GOD commendeth his love toward us, in that, while we were yet sinners, Christ died for us.

Much more then, being now justified by his blood, we shall be saved from wrath through him.

For if, when we were enemies, we were reconciled to God by the death of his Son, much more, being reconciled, we shall be saved by his life.

And not only so, but we also joy in God through our Lord Jesus Christ, by whom we have now received the atonement.

Romans 5:8-11

I THANK MY GOD upon every remembrance of you,

Always in every prayer of mine for you all making request with joy,

For your fellowship in the gospel from the first day until now;

Being confident of this very thing, that he which hath begun a good work in you will perform it until the day of Jesus Christ.

Philippians 1:3-6

I WILL both lay me down in peace, and sleep: for thou, Lord, only makest me dwell in safety.

Psalm 4:8

FOR THIS CAUSE we also, since the day we heard it, do not cease to pray for you, and to desire that ye might be filled with the knowledge of his will in all wisdom and spiritual understanding;

That ye might walk worthy of the Lord unto all pleasing, being fruitful in every good work, and increasing in the knowledge of God;

Strengthened with all might, according to his glorious power, unto all patience and longsuffering with joyfulness.

Colossians 1:9-11

FOR THE EYES of the Lord run to and fro throughout the whole earth, to shew himself strong in the behalf of them whose heart is perfect toward him . . . .

II Chronicles 16:9a

THE LORD taketh pleasure in them that fear him, in those that hope in his mercy.

Psalm 147:11

BLESSED BE THE GOD and Father of our Lord Jesus Christ, which according to his abundant mercy hath begotten us again unto a lively hope by the resurrection of Jesus Christ from the dead,

To an inheritance incorruptible, and undefiled, and that fadeth not away, reserved in heaven for you.

I Peter 1:3,4

MY SON, if thou wilt receive my words, and hide my commandments with thee;

So that thou incline thine ear unto wisdom, and apply thine heart to understanding;

Yea, if thou criest after knowledge, and liftest up thy voice for understanding;

If thou seekest her as silver, and searchest for her as for hid treasures;

Then shalt thou understand the fear of the Lord, and find the knowledge of God.

For the Lord giveth wisdom: out of his mouth cometh knowledge and understanding.

He layeth up sound wisdom for the righteous: he is a buckler to them that walk uprightly.

Proverbs 2:1-7

THROUGH GOD we shall do valiantly: for he it is that shall tread down our enemies.

Psalm 60:12

BLESSED IS THE MAN that trusteth in the Lord, and whose hope the Lord is.

For he shall be as a tree planted by the waters, and that spreadeth out her roots by the river, and shall not see when heat cometh, but her leaf shall be green; and shall not be careful in the year of drought, neither shall cease from yielding fruit.

Jeremiah 17:7,8

BUT IF WE WALK in the light, as he is in the light, we have fellowship one with another, and the blood of Jesus Christ his Son cleanseth us from all sin.

I John 1:7

IN MY DISTRESS I called upon the Lord, and cried unto my God: he heard my voice out of his temple, and my cry came before him, even into his ears.

Then the earth shook and trembled; the foundations also of the hills moved and were shaken, because he was wroth.

There went up a smoke out of his nostrils, and fire out of his mouth devoured: coals were kindled by it.

He bowed the heavens also, and came down: and darkness was under his feet.

And he rode upon a cherub, and did fly: yea, he did fly upon the wings of the wind.

He made darkness his secret place; his pavilion round about him were dark waters and thick clouds of the skies.

At the brightness that was before him his thick clouds passed, hail stones and coals of fire.

The Lord also thundered in the heavens, and the Highest gave his voice; hail stones and coals of fire.

Yea, he sent out his arrows, and scattered them; and he shot out lightnings, and discomfited them.

Then the channels of waters were seen, and the foundations of the world were discovered at thy rebuke, O Lord, at the blast of the breath of thy nostrils.

He sent from above, he took me, he drew me out of many waters.

He delivered me from my strong enemy, and from them which hated me: for they were too strong for me.

They prevented me in the day of my calamity: but the Lord was my stay.

He brought me forth also into a large place; he delivered me, because he delighted in me.

Psalm 18:6-19

THE LORD BLESS THEE, and keep thee:

The Lord make his face shine upon thee, and be gracious unto thee:

The Lord lift up his countenance upon thee, and give thee peace.

Numbers 6:24-26

AND IT SHALL come to pass, that before they call, I will answer; and while they are yet speaking, I will hear.

Isaiah 65:24

FOR THE LORD GOD is a sun and shield: the Lord will give grace and glory: no good thing will he withhold from them that walk uprightly.

Psalm 84:11

VERILY I SAY UNTO YOU, Whatsoever ye shall bind on earth shall be bound in heaven: and whatsoever ye shall loose on earth shall be loosed in heaven.

Again I say unto you, That if two of you shall agree on earth as touching any thing that they shall ask, it shall be done for them of my Father which is in heaven.

For where two or three are gathered together in my name, there am I in the midst of them.

Matthew 18:18-20

THIS BOOK OF THE LAW shall not depart out of thy mouth; but thou shalt meditate therein day and night, that thou mayest observe to do according to all that is written therein: for then thou shalt make thy way prosperous, and then thou shalt have good success.

Have not I commanded thee? Be strong and of a good courage; be not afraid, neither be thou dismayed: for the Lord thy God is with thee whithersoever thou goest.

Joshua 1:8,9

MANY, O LORD MY GOD, are thy wonderful works which thou hast done, and thy thoughts which are to usward: they cannot be reckoned up in order unto thee: if I would declare and speak of them, they are more than can be numbered.

Psalm 40:5

AND THE LORD, he it is that doth go before thee; he will be with thee, he will not fail thee, neither forsake thee: fear not, neither be dismayed.

Deuteronomy 31:8

AND WHEN DAVID inquired of the Lord, he said, Thou shalt not go up; but fetch a compass behind them, and come upon them over against the mulberry trees.

And let it be, when thou hearest the sound of a going in the tops of the mulberry trees, that then thou shalt bestir thyself: for then shall the Lord go out before thee, to smite the host of the Philistines.

II Samuel 5:23,24

HAPPY IS HE that hath the God of Jacob for his help, whose hope is in the Lord his God:

Which made heaven, and earth, the sea, and all that therein is: which keepeth truth for ever:

Which executeth judgment for the oppressed: which giveth food to the hungry. The Lord looseth the prisoners:

The Lord openeth the eyes of the blind: the Lord raiseth them that are bowed down: the Lord loveth the righteous:

The Lord preserveth the strangers; he relieveth the fatherless and widow: but the way of the wicked he turneth upside down.

The Lord shall reign for ever, even thy God, O Zion, unto all generations. Praise ye the Lord.

Psalm 146:5-10

BUT GOD, who is rich in mercy, for his great love wherewith he loved us,

Even when we were dead in sins, hath quickened us together with Christ, (by grace ye are saved;)

And hath raised us up together, and made us sit together in heavenly places in Christ Jesus:

That in the ages to come he might shew the exceeding riches of his grace in his kindness toward us through Christ Jesus.

For by grace are ye saved through faith; and that not of yourselves: it is the gift of God:

Not of works, lest any man should boast.

For we are his workmanship, created in Christ Jesus unto good works, which God hath before ordained that we should walk in them.

Ephesians 2:4-10

TO EVERY THING there is a season, and a time to every purpose under the heaven:

A time to be born, and a time to die; a time to plant, and a time to pluck up that which is planted;

A time to kill, and a time to heal; a time to break down, and a time to build up;

A time to weep, and a time to laugh; a time to mourn, and a time to dance;

A time to cast away stones, and a time to gather stones together; a time to embrace, and a time to refrain from embracing;

A time to get, and a time to lose; a time to keep, and a time to cast away;

A time to rend, and a time to sew; a time to keep silence, and a time to speak;

A time to love, and a time to hate; a time of war, and a time of peace.

What profit hath he that worketh in that wherein he laboureth?

I have seen the travail, which God hath given to the sons of men to be exercised in it.

He hath made every thing beautiful in his time: also he hath set the world in their heart, so that no man can find out the work that God maketh from the beginning to the end.

I know that there is no good in them, but for a man to rejoice, and to do good in his life.

And also that every man should eat and drink, and enjoy the good of all his labour, it is the gift of God.

Ecclesiastes 3:1-13

THE LORD is gracious, and full of compassion; slow to anger, and of great mercy.

The Lord is good to all: and his tender mercies are over all his works.

All thy works shall praise thee, O Lord; and thy saints shall bless thee.

Psalm 145:8-10

IF MY PEOPLE, which are called by my name, shall humble themselves, and pray, and seek my face, and turn from their wicked ways; then will I hear from heaven, and will forgive their sin, and will heal their land.

II Chronicles 7:14

REMEMBER, I BESEECH THEE, the word that thou commandedst thy servant Moses, saying, If ye transgress, I will scatter you abroad among the nations:

But if ye turn unto me, and keep my commandments, and do them; though there were of you cast out unto the uttermost part of the heaven, yet will I gather them from thence, and will bring them unto the place that I have chosen to set my name there.

Nehemiah 1:8,9

THE LORD is my light and my salvation; whom shall I fear? the Lord is the strength of my life; of whom shall I be afraid?

When the wicked, even mine enemies and my foes, came upon me to eat up my flesh, they stumbled and fell.

Though an host should encamp against me, my heart shall not fear: though war should rise against me, in this will I be confident.

Psalm 27:1-3

NEITHER PRAY I for these alone, but for them also which shall believe on me through their word;

That they all may be one; as thou, Father, art in me, and I in thee, that they also may be one in us that the world may believe that thou hast sent me.

And the glory which thou gavest me I have given them; that they may be one, even as we are one:

I in them, and thou in me, that they may be made perfect in one; and that the world may know that thou hast sent me, and hast loved them, as thou hast loved me.

John 17:20-23

SEEING THEN that we have a great high priest, that is passed into the heavens, Jesus the Son of God, let us hold fast our profession.

For we have not an high priest which cannot be touched with the feeling of our infirmities; but was in all points tempted like as we are, yet without sin.

Let us therefore come boldly unto the throne of grace, that we may obtain mercy, and find grace to help in time of need.

Hebrews 4:14-16

I WILL LIFT UP mine eyes unto the hills, from whence cometh my help.

My help cometh from the Lord, which made heaven and earth.

He will not suffer thy foot to be moved: he that keepeth thee will not slumber.

Behold, he that keepeth Israel shall neither slumber nor sleep.

The Lord is thy keeper: the Lord is thy shade upon thy right hand.

The sun shall not smite thee by day, nor the moon by night.

The Lord shall preserve thee from all evil: he shall preserve thy soul.

The Lord shall preserve thy going out and thy coming in from this time forth, and even for evermore.

Psalm 121

AND HE CRIED unto the Lord; and the Lord showed him a tree, which when he had cast into the waters, the waters were made sweet: there he made for them a statute and an ordinance, and there he proved them,

And said, If thou wilt diligently hearken to the voice of the Lord thy God, and wilt do that which is right in his sight, and wilt give ear to his commandments, and keep all his statutes, I will put none of these diseases upon thee, which I have brought upon the Egyptians: for I am the Lord that healeth thee.

Exodus 15:25,26

HEAL ME, O LORD, and I shall be healed; save me, and I shall be saved: for thou art my praise.

Jeremiah 17:14

THEY THAT GO DOWN to the sea in ships, that do business in great waters;

These see the works of the Lord, and his wonders in the deep.

For he commandeth, and raiseth the stormy wind, which lifteth up the waves thereof.

They mount up to the heaven, they go down again to the depths: their soul is melted because of trouble.

They reel to and fro, and stagger like a drunken man, and are at their wit's end.

Then they cry unto the Lord in their trouble, and he bringeth them out of their distresses.

He maketh the storm a calm, so that the waves thereof are still.

Then are they glad because they be quiet; so he bringeth them unto their desired haven.

Oh that men would praise the Lord for his goodness, and for his wonderful works to the children of men!

Let them exalt him also in the congregation of the people, and praise him in the assembly of the elders.

Psalm 107:23-32

THERE IS therefore now no condemnation to them which are in Christ Jesus, who walk not after the flesh, but after the Spirit.

For the law of the Spirit of life in Christ Jesus hath made me free from the law of sin and death.

Romans 8:1,2

YE HAVE HEARD that it hath been said, Thou shalt love thy neighbour, and hate thine enemy.

But I say unto you, Love your enemies, bless them that curse you, do good to them that hate you, and pray for them which despitefully use you, and persecute you;

That ye may be the children of your Father which is in heaven: for he maketh his sun to rise on the evil and on the good, and sendeth rain on the just and on the unjust.

For if you love them which love you, what reward have ye? do not even the publicans the same?

And if ye salute your brethren only, what do ye more than others? do not even the publicans so?

Be ye therefore perfect, even as your Father which is in heaven is perfect.

Matthew 5:43-48

THE LORD doth build up Jerusalem: he gathereth together the outcasts of Israel.

He healeth the broken in heart, and bindeth up their wounds.

He telleth the number of the stars; he calleth them all by their names.

Great is our Lord, and of great power: his understanding is infinite.

Psalm 147:2-5

AND IN THAT DAY thou shalt say, O Lord, I will praise thee: though thou wast angry with me, thine anger is turned away, and thou comfortedst me.

Behold, God is my salvation I will trust, and not be afraid: for the Lord JEHOVAH is my strength and my song; he also is become my salvation.

Therefore with joy shall ye draw water out of the wells of salvation.

Isaiah 12:1-3

AND THE LORD SAID unto Moses, Is the Lord's hand waxed short? thou shalt see now whether my word shall come to pass unto thee or not.

Numbers 11:23

BLESSED BE THE LORD because he hath heard the voice of my supplications.

The Lord is my strength and my shield; my heart trusted in him, and I am helped: therefore my heart greatly rejoiceth; and with my song will I praise him.

The Lord is their strength, and he is the saving strength of his anointed.

Psalm 28:6-8

FOR ALL THINGS are for your sakes, that the abundant grace might through the thanksgiving of many redound to the glory of God.

For which cause we faint not; but though our outward man perish, yet the inward man is renewed day by day.

For our light affliction, which is but for a moment, worketh for us a far more exceeding and eternal weight of glory;

While we look not at the things which are seen, but at the things which are not seen: for the things which are seen are temporal; but the things which are not seen are eternal.

II Corinthians 4:15-18

WHEN THOU PASSEST through the waters, I will be with thee; and through the rivers, they shall not overflow thee: when thou walkest through the fire, thou shalt not be burned; neither shall the flame kindle upon thee.

For I am the Lord thy God, the Holy One of Israel, thy Saviour: I gave Egypt for thy ransom, Ethiopia and Seba for thee.

Since thou wast precious in my sight, thou hast been honourable, and I have loved thee: therefore will I give men for thee, and people for thy life.

Fear not: for I am with thee: I will bring thy seed from the east, and gather thee from the west;

I will say to the north, Give up; and to the south, Keep not back: bring my sons from far, and my daughters from the ends of the earth;

Even every one that is called by my name: for I have created him for my glory, I have formed him; yea, I have made him.

Isaiah 43:2-7

I WILL instruct thee and teach thee in the way which thou shalt go: I will guide thee with mine eye.

Psalm 32:8

IF WE CONFESS our sins, he is faithful and just to forgive us our sins, and to cleanse us from all unrighteousness.

I John 1:9

I THANK MY GOD always on your behalf, for the grace of God which is given you by Jesus Christ;

That in every thing ye are enriched by him, in all utterance, and in all knowledge;

Even as the testimony of Christ was confirmed in you:

So that ye come behind in no gift; waiting for the coming of our Lord Jesus Christ:

Who shall also confirm you unto the end, that ye may be blameless in the day of our Lord Jesus Christ.

God is faithful, by whom ye were called unto the fellowship of his Son Jesus Christ our Lord.

I Corinthians 1:4-9

I WILL HEAR what God the Lord will speak: for he will speak peace unto his people, and to his saints: but let them not turn again to folly.

Surely his salvation is nigh them that fear him; that glory may dwell in our land.

Mercy and truth are met together; righteousness and peace have kissed each other.

Truth shall spring out of the earth; and righteousness shall look down from heaven.

Yea, the Lord shall give that which is good; and our land shall yield her increase.

Righteousness shall go before him; and shall set us in the way of his steps.

Psalm 85:8-13

AND HE SAID to them all, If any man will come after me, let him deny himself, and take up his cross daily, and follow me.

For whosoever will save his life shall lose it: but whosoever will lose his life for my sake, the same shall save it.

Luke 9:23,24

LET NOT MERCY and truth forsake thee: bind them about thy neck; write them upon the table of thine heart:

So shalt thou find favour and good understanding in the sight of God and man.

Proverbs 3:3,4

BE MERCIFUL unto me, O God, be merciful unto me: for my soul trusteth in thee: yea, in the shadow of thy wings will I make my refuge, until these calamities be overpast.

I will cry unto God most high; unto God that performeth all things for me.

He shall send from heaven, and save me from the reproach of him that would swallow me up. Selah. God shall send forth his mercy and his truth.

Psalm 57:1-3

THE ETERNAL GOD is thy refuge, and underneath are the everlasting arms . . . .

Deuteronomy 33:27a

HE THAT HATH an ear, let him hear what the Spirit saith unto the churches; To him that overcometh will I give to eat of the tree of life, which is in the midst of the paradise of God.

Revelation 2:7

SHEW THY MARVELLOUS loving-kindness, O thou that savest by thy right hand them which put their trust in thee from those that rise up against them.

Psalm 17:7

FOR IT IS GOD which worketh in you both to will and to do of his good pleasure.

Philippians 2:13

FORASMUCH AS YE know that ye were not redeemed with corruptible things, as silver and gold, from your vain conversation received by tradition from your fathers;

But with the precious blood of Christ, as of a lamb without blemish and without spot:

Who verily was foreordained before the foundation of the world, but was manifest in these last times for you.

I Peter 1:18-20

O LORD MY GOD, I cried unto thee, and thou hast healed me.

O Lord, thou hast brought up my soul from the grave: thou hast kept me alive, that I should not go down to the pit.

Psalm 30:2,3

THEREFORE I SAY unto you, Take no thought for your life, what ye shall eat, or what ye shall drink; nor yet for your body, what ye shall put on. Is not the life more than meat, and the body than raiment?

Behold the fowls of the air: for they sow not, neither do they reap, nor gather into barns; yet your heavenly Father feedeth them. Are ye not much better than they?

Which of you by taking thought can add one cubit unto his stature?

And why take ye thought for raiment? Consider the lilies of the field, how they grow; they toil not, neither do they spin:

And yet I say unto you, That even Solomon in all his glory was not arrayed like one of these.

Wherefore, if God so clothe the grass of the field, which today is, and to morrow is cast into the oven, shall he not much more clothe you, O ye of little faith?

Therefore take no thought, saying, What shall we eat? or, What shall we drink? or, Wherewithal shall we be clothed?

(For after all these things do the Gentiles seek:) for your heavenly Father knoweth that ye have need of all these things.

But seek ye first the kingdom of God, and his righteousness; and all these things shall be added unto you.

Take therefore no thought for the morrow: for the morrow shall take thought for the things of itself. Sufficient unto the day is the evil thereof.

Matthew 6:25-34

THE NEXT DAY John seeth Jesus coming unto him, and saith, Behold the Lamb of God, which taketh away the sin of the world.

John 1:29

HEAR ME, O LORD; for thy lovingkindness is good: turn unto me according to the multitude of thy tender mercies.

And hide not thy face from thy servant; for I am in trouble: hear me speedily.

Psalm 69:16,17

AND THE LORD said unto Joshua, This day will I begin to magnify thee in the sight of all Israel, that they may know that, as I was with Moses, so I will be with thee.

Joshua 3:7

LET US HEAR the conclusion of the whole matter: Fear God, and keep his commandments: for this is the whole duty of man.

For God shall bring every work into judgment, with every secret thing, whether it be good, or whether it be evil.

Ecclesiastes 12:13,14

I SOUGHT THE LORD, and he heard me, and delivered me from all my fears.

They looked unto him, and were lightened: and their faces were not ashamed.

This poor man cried, and the Lord heard him, and saved him out of all his troubles.

The angel of the Lord encampeth round about them that fear him, and delivereth them.

Psalm 34:4-7

HE TRUSTED in the Lord God of Israel; so that after him was none like him among all the kings of Judah, nor any that were before him.

For he clave to the Lord, and departed not from following him, but kept his commandments, which the Lord commanded Moses.

And the Lord was with him; and he prospered whithersoever he went forth: and he rebelled against the king of Assyria, and served him not.

II Kings 18:5-7

HEAR THE WORD of the Lord, ye that tremble at his word; Your brethren that hated you, that cast you out for my name's sake, said, Let the Lord be glorified: but he shall appear to your joy, and they shall be ashamed.

Isaiah 66:5

O GIVE THANKS unto the Lord; for he is good: because his mercy endureth for ever.

Let Israel now say, that his mercy endureth for ever.

Let the house of Aaron now say, that his mercy endureth for ever.

Let them now that fear the Lord say, that his mercy endureth for ever.

I called upon the Lord in distress: the Lord answered me, and set me in a large place.

The Lord is on my side; I will not fear: what can man do unto me?

Psalm 118:1-6

IN MY DISTRESS I called upon the Lord, and cried to my God: and he did hear my voice out of his temple, and my cry did enter into his ears.

II Samuel 22:7

A NEW HEART ALSO will I give you, and a new spirit will I put within you: and I will take away the stony heart out of your flesh, and I will give you an heart of flesh.

And I will put my spirit within you, and cause you to walk in my statutes, and ye shall keep my judgments, and do them.

Ezekiel 36:26,27

ARE THEY not all ministering spirits, sent forth to minister for them who shall be heirs of salvation?

Hebrews 1:14

AS THOU KNOWEST NOT what is the way of the spirit, nor how the bones do grow in the womb of her that is with child: even so thou knowest not the works of God who maketh all.

In the morning sow thy seed, and in the evening withhold not thine hand: for thou knowest not whether shall prosper, either this or that, or whether they both shall be alike good.

Ecclesiastes 11:5,6

WHEREFORE I ALSO, after I heard of your faith in the Lord Jesus, and love unto all the saints,

Cease not to give thanks for you, making mention of you in my prayers,

That the God of our Lord Jesus Christ, the Father of glory, may give unto you the spirit of wisdom and revelation in the knowledge of him:

The eyes of your understanding being enlightened; that ye may know what is the hope of his calling, and what the riches of the glory of his inheritance in the saints,

And what is the exceeding greatness of his power to usward who believe, according to the working of his mighty power,

Which he wrought in Christ, when he raised him from the dead, and set him at his own right hand in the heavenly places,

Far above all principality, and power, and might, and dominion, and every name that is named, not only in this world, but also in that which is to come:

And hath put all things under his feet, and gave him to be the head over all things to the church,

Which is his body, the fulness of him that filleth all in all.

Ephesians 1:15-23

THE LORD upholdeth all that fall, and raiseth up all those that be bowed down.

The eyes of all wait upon thee; and thou givest them their meat in due season.

Thou openest thine hand, and satisfiest the desire of every living thing.

The Lord is righteous in all his ways, and holy in all his works.

The Lord is nigh unto all them that call upon him, to all that call upon him in truth.

He will fulfil the desire of them that fear him: he also will hear their cry, and will save them.

The Lord preserveth all them that love him: but all the wicked will he destroy.

My mouth shall speak the praise of the Lord: and let all flesh bless his holy name for ever and ever.

Psalm 145:14-21

MY LITTLE CHILDREN, these things write I unto you, that ye sin not. And if any man sin, we have an advocate with the Father, Jesus Christ the righteous:

And he is the propitiation for our sins: and not for ours only, but also for the sins of the whole world.

I John 2:1,2

THEN SAID I UNTO THEM, Ye see the distress that we are in, how Jerusalem lieth waste, and the gates thereof are burned with fire: come, and let us build up the wall of Jerusalem, that we be no more a reproach.

Then I told them of the hand of my God which was good upon me; as also the king's words that he had spoken unto me. And they said, Let us rise up and build. So they strengthened their hands for this good work.

Nehemiah 2:17,18

TRUST IN THE LORD, and do good; so shalt thou dwell in the land, and verily thou shalt be fed.

Delight thyself also in the Lord; and he shall give thee the desires of thine heart.

Commit thy way unto the Lord; trust also in him, and he shall bring it to pass.

And he shall bring forth thy righteousness as the light, and thy judgment as the noonday.

Rest in the Lord, and wait patiently for him . . . .

Psalm 37:3-7a

ASK, and it shall be given you; seek, and ye shall find; knock, and it shall be opened unto you:

For every one that asketh receiveth; and he that seeketh findeth; and to him that knocketh it shall be opened.

Or what man is there of you, whom if his son ask bread, will he give him a stone?

Or if he ask a fish, will he give him a serpent?

If ye then, being evil, know how to give good gifts unto your children, how much more shall your Father which is in heaven give good things to them that ask him?

Matthew 7:7-11

FOR THE EARTH shall be filled with the knowledge of the glory of the Lord, as the waters cover the sea.

Habakkuk 2:14

FOR THE PREACHING of the cross is to them that perish foolishness; but unto us which are saved it is the power of God.

I Corinthians 1:18

I REJOICE at thy word, as one that findeth great spoil.

Psalm 119:162

BUT YE ARE a chosen generation, a royal priesthood, an holy nation, a peculiar people; that ye should shew forth the praises of him who hath called you out of darkness into his marvellous light.

I Peter 2:9

O LORD, thou art my God; I will exalt thee, I will praise thy name; for thou hast done wonderful things; thy counsels of old are faithfulness and truth.

For thou hast made of a city an heap; of a defenced city a ruin: a palace of strangers to be no city; it shall never be built.

Therefore shall the strong people glorify thee, the city of the terrible nations shall fear thee.

For thou hast been a strength to the poor, a strength to the needy in his distress, a refuge from the storm, a shadow from the heat, when the blast of the terrible ones is as a storm against the wall.

Isaiah 25:1-4

IN THEE, O LORD, do I put my trust: let me never be put to confusion.

Deliver me in thy righteousness, and cause me to escape: incline thine ear unto me, and save me.

Be thou my strong habitation, whereunto I may continually resort: thou hast given commandment to save me; for thou art my rock and my fortress.

Psalm 71:1-3

IF THAT NATION, against whom I have pronounced, turn from their evil, I will repent of the evil that I thought to do unto them.

Jeremiah 18:8

BEWARE lest any man spoil you through philosophy and vain deceit, after the tradition of men, after the rudiments of the world, and not after Christ.

For in him dwelleth all the fulness of the Godhead bodily.

And ye are complete in him, which is the head of all principality and power.

Colossians 2:8-10

FOR THOU, LORD, art good, and ready to forgive; and plenteous in mercy unto all them that call upon thee.

Psalm 86:5

JESUS ANSWERED and said unto her, Whosoever drinketh of this water shall thirst again:

But whosoever drinketh of the water that I shall give him shall never thirst; but the water that I shall give him shall be in him a well of water springing up into everlasting life.

John 4:13,14

HONOUR THE LORD with thy substance, and with the firstfruits of all thine increase:

So shall thy barns be filled with plenty, and thy presses shall burst out with new wine.

Proverbs 3:9,10

O GIVE THANKS unto the Lord; call upon his name: make known his deeds among the people.

Sing unto him, sing psalms unto him: talk ye of all his wondrous works.

Glory ye in his holy name: let the heart of them rejoice that seek the Lord.

Seek the Lord, and his strength: seek his face evermore.

Remember his marvellous works that he hath done; his wonders, and the judgments of his mouth;

O ye seed of Abraham his servant, ye children of Jacob his chosen.

He is the Lord our God: his judgments are in all the earth.

He hath remembered his covenant for ever, the word which he commanded to a thousand generations.

Which covenant he made with Abraham, and his oath unto Isaac;

And confirmed the same unto Jacob for a law, and to Israel for an everlasting covenant:

Saying, Unto thee will I give the land of Canaan, the lot of your inheritance:

When they were but a few men in number; yea, very few, and strangers in it.

When they went from one nation to another, from one kingdom to another people;

He suffered no man to do them wrong: yea, he reproved kings for their sakes;

Saying, Touch not mine anointed, and do my prophets no harm.

Moreover he called for a famine upon the land: he brake the whole staff of bread.

He sent a man before them, even Joseph, who was sold for a servant:

Whose feet they hurt with fetters: he was laid in iron:

Until the time that his word came: the word of the Lord tried him.

The king sent and loosed him; even the ruler of the people, and let him go free.

He made him lord of his house, and ruler of all his substance:

To bind his princes at his pleasure; and teach his senators wisdom.

Israel also came into Egypt; and Jacob sojourned in the land of Ham.

And he increased his people greatly; and made them stronger than their enemies.

He turned their heart to hate his people, to deal subtilly with his servants.

He sent Moses his servant; and Aaron whom he had chosen.

They shewed his signs among them, and wonders in the land of Ham.

He sent darkness, and made it dark; and they rebelled not against his word.

He turned their waters into blood, and slew their fish.

Their land brought forth frogs in abundance, in the chambers of their kings.

He spake, and there came divers sorts of flies, and lice in all their coasts.

He gave them hail for rain, and flaming fire in their land.

He smote their vines also and their fig trees; and brake the trees of their coasts.

He spake, and the locusts came, and caterpillers, and that without number,

And did eat up all the herbs in their land, and devoured the fruit of their ground.

He smote also all the firstborn in their land, the chief of all their strength.

He brought them forth also with silver and gold: and there was not one feeble person among their tribes.

Egypt was glad when they departed: for the fear of them fell upon them.

He spread a cloud for a covering; and fire to give light in the night.

The people asked, and he brought quails,

and satisfied them with the bread of heaven.

He opened the rock, and the waters gushed out; they ran in the dry places like a river.

For he remembered his holy promise, and Abraham his servant.

And he brought forth his people with joy, and his chosen with gladness:

And gave them the lands of the heathen: and they inherited the labour of the people;

That they might observe his statutes, and keep his laws. Praise ye the Lord.

Psalm 105

BUT WHAT THINGS were gain to me, those I counted loss for Christ.

Yea doubtless, and I count all things but loss for the excellency of the knowledge of Christ Jesus my Lord: for whom I have suffered the loss of all things, and do count them but dung, that I may win Christ,

And be found in him, not having mine own righteousness, which is of the law, but that which is through the faith of Christ, the righteousness which is of God by faith.

Philippians 3:7-9

I EXHORT therefore, that, first of all, supplications, prayers, intercessions, and giving of thanks, be made for all men;

For kings, and for all that are in authority; that we may lead a quiet and peaceable life in all godliness and honesty.

For this is good and acceptable in the sight of God our Saviour;

Who will have all men to be saved, and to come unto the knowledge of the truth.

I Timothy 2:1-4

WHEN I CRY unto thee, then shall mine enemies turn back: this I know; for God is for me.

In God will I praise his word: in the Lord will I praise his word.

In God have I put my trust: I will not be afraid what man can do unto me.

Psalm 56:9-11

FOR WHOSOEVER exalteth himself shall be abased; and he that humbleth himself shall be exalted.

Luke 14:11

LIKEWISE the Spirit also helpeth our infirmities: for we know not what we should pray for as we ought: but the Spirit itself maketh intercession for us with groanings which cannot be uttered.

And he that searcheth the hearts knoweth what is the mind of the Spirit, because he maketh intercession for the saints according to the will of God.

And we know that all things work together for good to them that love God, to them who are the called according to his purpose.

Romans 8:26-28

WHAT MAN is he that feareth the Lord? him shall he teach in the way that he shall choose.

His soul shall dwell at ease; and his seed shall inherit the earth.

The secret of the Lord is with them that fear him; and he will shew them his covenant.

Psalm 25:12-14

AND MOSES SAID unto the people, Fear ye not, stand still, and see the salvation of the Lord, which he will shew to you today: for the Egyptians whom ye have seen today, ye shall see them again no more for ever.

The Lord shall fight for you, and ye shall hold your peace.

Exodus 14:13,14

JESUS ANSWERED and said unto them, Verily I say unto you, If ye have faith, and doubt not, ye shall not only do this which is done to the fig tree, but also if ye shall say unto this mountain, Be thou removed, and be thou cast into the sea; it shall be done.

And all things, whatsoever ye shall ask in prayer, believing, ye shall receive.

Matthew 21:21,22

THE LORD is my rock, and my fortress, and my deliverer; my God, my strength, in whom I will trust; my buckler, and the horn of my salvation, and my high tower.

I will call upon the Lord, who is worthy to be praised: so shall I be saved from mine enemies.

Psalm 18:2,3

THEREFORE if any man be in Christ, he is a new creature: old things are passed away; behold, all things are become new.

II Corinthians 5:17

WITH THE MERCIFUL thou wilt shew thyself merciful, and with the upright man thou wilt shew thyself upright.

With the pure thou wilt shew thyself pure; and with the froward thou wilt shew thyself unsavoury

And the afflicted people thou wilt save: but thine eyes are upon the haughty, that thou mayest bring them down.

For thou art my lamp, O Lord: and the Lord will lighten my darkness.

For by thee I have run through a troop: by my God have I leaped over a wall.

II Samuel 22:26-30

NEVERTHELESS I AM continually with thee: thou hast holden me by my right hand.

Thou shalt guide me with thy counsel, and afterward receive me to glory

Whom have I in heaven but thee? and there is none upon earth that I desire beside thee.

My flesh and my heart faileth: but God is the strength of my heart, and my portion for ever.

Psalm 73:23-26

FOR WHEN YE were the servants of sin, ye were free from righteousness.

What fruit had ye then in those things whereof ye are now ashamed? for the end of those things is death.

But now being made free from sin, and become servants to God, ye have your fruit unto holiness, and the end everlasting life.

For the wages of sin is death; but the gift of God is eternal life through Jesus Christ our Lord.

Romans 6:20-23

FEAR NOT; for thou shalt not be ashamed: neither be thou confounded; for thou shalt not be put to shame: for thou shalt forget the shame of thy youth, and shalt not remember the reproach of thy widowhood any more.

For thy Maker is thine husband; the Lord of hosts is his name; and thy Redeemer the Holy One of Israel; The God of the whole earth shall he be called.

For the Lord hath called thee as a woman forsaken and grieved in spirit, and a wife of youth, when thou wast refused, saith thy God.

For a small moment have I forsaken thee; but with great mercies will I gather thee.

In a little wrath I hid my face from thee for a moment; but with everlasting kindness will I have mercy on thee, saith the Lord thy Redeemer.

For this is as the waters of Noah unto me: for as I have sworn that the waters of Noah should no more go over the earth; so have I sworn that I would not be wroth with thee, nor rebuke thee.

For the mountains shall depart, and the hills be removed; but my kindness shall not depart from thee, neither shall the covenant of my peace be removed, saith the Lord that hath mercy on thee.

O thou afflicted, tossed with tempest, and not comforted, behold, I will lay thy stones with fair colours, and lay thy foundations with sapphires.

And I will make thy windows of agates, and thy gates of carbuncles, and all thy borders of pleasant stones.

And all thy children shall be taught of the Lord; and great shall be the peace of thy children.

In righteousness shalt thou be established: thou shalt be far from oppression; for thou shalt not fear: and from terror; for it shall not come near thee.

Behold, they shall surely gather together, but not by me: whosoever shall gather together against thee shall fall for thy sake.

Behold, I have created the smith that bloweth the coals in the fire, and that bringeth forth an instrument for his work; and I have created the waster to destroy.

No weapon that is formed against thee shall prosper; and every tongue that shall rise against thee in judgment thou shalt condemn. This is the heritage of the servants of the Lord, and their righteousness is of me, saith the Lord.

Isaiah 54:4-17

SING UNTO THE LORD, O ye saints of his, and give thanks at the remembrance of his holiness.

For his anger endureth but a moment; in his favour is life: weeping may endure for a night, but joy cometh in the morning.

Psalm 30:4,5

THEN I SAID unto you, Dread not, neither be afraid of them.

The Lord your God which goeth before you, he shall fight for you, according to all that he did for you in Egypt before your eyes.

Deuteronomy 1:29,30

PEACE I LEAVE WITH YOU, my peace I give unto you: not as the world giveth, give I unto you. Let not your heart be troubled, neither let it be afraid.

John 14:27

CAST ME NOT OFF in the time of old age; forsake me not when my strength faileth.

For mine enemies speak against me; and they that lay wait for my soul take counsel together,

Saying, God hath forsaken him: persecute and take him; for there is none to deliver him.

O God, be not far from me: O my God, make haste for my help.

Let them be confounded and consumed that are adversaries to my soul; let them be covered with reproach and dishonour that seek my hurt.

But I will hope continually, and will yet praise thee more and more.

My mouth shall shew forth thy righteousness and thy salvation all the day; for I know not the numbers thereof.

I will go in the strength of the Lord GOD: I will make mention of thy righteousness, even of thine only.

O God, thou hast taught me from my youth: and hitherto have I declared thy wondrous works.

Now also when I am old and greyheaded, O God, forsake me not; until I have shewed thy strength unto this generation, and thy power to every one that is to come.

Psalm 71:9-18

BUT THIS MAN, because he continueth ever, hath an unchangeable priesthood.

Wherefore he is able also to save them to the uttermost that come unto God by him, seeing he ever liveth to make intercession for them.

Hebrews 7:24,25

HE THAT HATH an ear, let him hear what the Spirit saith unto the churches; To him that overcometh will I give to eat of the hidden manna, and will give him a white stone, and in the stone a new name written, which no man knoweth saving he that receiveth it.

Revelation 2:17

O PRAISE THE LORD, all ye nations: praise him, all ye people.

For his merciful kindness is great toward us: and the truth of the Lord endureth for ever. Praise ye the Lord.

Psalm 117

AND JOSHUA SAID unto the children of Israel, Come hither, and hear the words of the Lord your God.

And Joshua said, Hereby ye shall know that the living God is among you, and that he will without fail drive out from before you the Canaanites, and the Hittites, and the Hivites, and the Perizzites, and the Girgashites, and the Amorites, and the Jebusites.

Joshua 3:9,10

FINALLY, MY BRETHREN, be strong in the Lord, and in the power of his might.

Put on the whole armour of God, that ye may be able to stand against the wiles of the devil.

For we wrestle not against flesh and blood, but against principalities, against powers, against the rulers of the darkness of this world, against spiritual wickedness in high places.

Wherefore take unto you the whole armour of God, that ye may be able to withstand in the evil day, and having done all to stand.

Stand therefore, having your loins girt about with truth, and having on the breastplate of righteousness;

And your feet shod with the preparation of the gospel of peace;

Above all, taking the shield of faith, wherewith ye shall be able to quench all the fiery darts of the wicked.

And take the helmet of salvation, and the sword of the Spirit, which is the word of God:

Praying always with all prayer and supplication in the Spirit, and watching thereunto with all perseverance and supplication for all saints.

Ephesians 6:10-18

I LOVE THE LORD, because he hath heard my voice and my supplications.

Because he hath inclined his ear unto me, therefore will I call upon him as long as I live.

The sorrows of death compassed me, and the pains of hell gat hold upon me: I found trouble and sorrow.

Then called I upon the name of the Lord; O Lord, I beseech thee, deliver my soul.

Gracious is the Lord, and righteous; yea, our God is merciful.

The Lord preserveth the simple: I was brought low, and he helped me.

Return unto thy rest, O my soul; for the Lord hath dealt bountifully with thee.

For thou hast delivered my soul from death, mine eyes from tears, and my feet from falling.

I will walk before the Lord in the land of the living.

Psalm 116:1-9

THEN THE KING commanded, and they brought Daniel, and cast him into the den of lions. Now the king spake and said unto Daniel, Thy God whom thou servest continually, he will deliver thee.

Daniel 6:16

AND I LOOKED, and rose up, and said unto the nobles, and to the rulers, and to the rest of the people, Be not ye afraid of them: remember the Lord, which is great and terrible, and fight for your brethren, your sons, and your daughters, your wives, and your houses.

And it came to pass, when our enemies heard that it was known unto us, and God had brought their counsel to nought, that we returned all of us to the wall, every one unto his work.

Nehemiah 4:14,15

GOOD AND UPRIGHT is the Lord: therefore will he teach sinners in the way.

The meek will he guide in judgment: and the meek will he teach his way.

All the paths of the Lord are mercy and truth unto such as keep his covenant and his testimonies.

Psalm 25:8-10

HE THAT OVERCOMETH, the same shall be clothed in white raiment; and I will not blot out his name out of the book of life, but I will confess his name before my Father, and before his angels.

Revelation 3:5

FOR THE KINGDOM OF GOD is not meat and drink; but righteousness, and peace, and joy in the Holy Ghost.

Romans 14:17

BLESSED BE THE LORD my strength, which teacheth my hands to war, and my fingers to fight:

My goodness, and my fortress; my high tower, and my deliverer; my shield, and he in whom I trust; who subdueth my people under me.

Psalm 144:1,2

THEN SAID JESUS to those Jews which believed on him, If ye continue in my word, then are ye my disciples indeed;

And ye shall know the truth, and the truth shall make you free.

John 8:31,32

BUT WHEN they deliver you up, take no thought how or what ye shall speak: for it shall be given you in that same hour what ye shall speak.

For it is not ye that speak, but the Spirit of your Father which speaketh in you.

Matthew 10:19,20

O LOVE THE LORD, all ye his saints: for the Lord preserveth the faithful, and plentifully rewardeth the proud doer.

Be of good courage, and he shall strengthen your heart, all ye that hope in the Lord.

Psalm 31:23,24

AND HE SAID, The Lord is my rock, and my fortress, and my deliverer;

The God of my rock; in him will I trust: he is my shield, and the horn of my salvation, my high tower, and my refuge, my saviour; thou savest me from violence.

I will call on the Lord, who is worthy to be praised: so shall I be saved from mine enemies.

II Samuel 22:2-4

BELOVED, think it not strange concerning the fiery trial which is to try you, as though some strange thing happened unto you:

But rejoice, inasmuch as ye are partakers of Christ's sufferings; that, when his glory shall be revealed, ye may be glad also with exceeding joy.

If ye be reproached for the name of Christ, happy are ye; for the spirit of glory and of God resteth upon you: on their part he is evil spoken of, but on your part he is glorified.

I Peter 4:12-14

HE TURNETH RIVERS into a wilderness, and the watersprings into dry ground;

A fruitful land into barrenness, for the wickedness of them that dwell therein.

He turneth the wilderness into a standing water, and dry ground into watersprings.

And there he maketh the hungry to dwell, that they may prepare a city for habitation;

And sow the fields, and plant vineyards, which may yield fruits of increase.

He blesseth them also, so that they are multiplied greatly; and suffereth not their cattle to decrease.

Again, they are minished and brought low through oppression, affliction, and sorrow.

He poureth contempt upon princes, and causeth them to wander in the wilderness, where there is no way.

Yet setteth he the poor on high from affliction, and maketh him families like a flock.

The righteous shall see it, and rejoice: and all iniquity shall stop her mouth.

Whoso is wise, and will observe these things, even they shall understand the lovingkindness of the Lord.

Psalm 107:33-43

BUT WHOSO keepeth his word, in him verily is the love of God perfected: hereby know we that we are in him.

I John 2:5

WHAT? know ye not that your body is the temple of the Holy Ghost which is in you, which ye have of God, and ye are not your own?

For ye are bought with a price: therefore glorify God in your body, and in your spirit, which are God's.

I Corinthians 6:19,20

BRING YE all the tithes into the storehouse, that there may be meat in mine house, and prove me now herewith, saith the Lord of hosts, if I will not open you the windows of heaven, and pour you out a blessing, that there shall not be room enough to receive it.

And I will rebuke the devourer for your sakes, and he shall not destroy the fruits of your ground; neither shall your vine cast her fruit before the time in the field, saith the Lord of hosts.

Malachi 3:10,11

AND IN THIS MOUNTAIN shall the Lord of hosts make unto all people a feast of fat things, a feast of wines on the lees, of fat things full of marrow, of wines on the lees well refined.

And he will destroy in this mountain the face of the covering cast over all people, and the veil that is spread over all nations.

He will swallow up death in victory; and the Lord GOD will wipe away tears from off all faces; and the rebuke of his people shall he take away from off all the earth: for the Lord hath spoken it.

And it shall be said in that day, Lo, this is our God; we have waited for him, and he will save us: this is the Lord; we have waited for him, we will be glad and rejoice in his salvation.

Isaiah 25:6-9

MY SON, despise not the chastening of the Lord; neither be weary of his correction:
For whom the Lord loveth he correcteth; even as a father the son in whom he delighteth.

Proverbs 3:11,12

THE ENTRANCE of thy words giveth light; it giveth understanding unto the simple.

Psalm 119:130

CAST THY BREAD upon the waters: for thou shalt find it after many days.

Ecclesiastes 11:1

BRETHREN, I count not myself to have apprehended: but this one thing I do, forgetting those things which are behind, and reaching forth unto those things which are before,
I press toward the mark for the prize of the high calling of God in Christ Jesus.

Let us therefore, as many as be perfect, be thus minded: and if in any thing ye be otherwise minded, God shall reveal even this unto you.

Philippians 3:13-15

BLESSED IS HE that considereth the poor: the Lord will deliver him in time of trouble.

The Lord will preserve him, and keep him alive; and he shall be blessed upon the earth: and thou wilt not deliver him unto the will of his enemies.

Psalm 41:1,2

FOR CHRIST is not entered into the holy places made with hands, which are the figures of the true; but into heaven itself, now to appear in the presence of God for us.

Hebrews 9:24

LIKEWISE, I SAY unto you, there is joy in the presence of the angels of God over one sinner that repenteth.

Luke 15:10

TRULY MY SOUL waiteth upon God: from him cometh my salvation.

He only is my rock and my salvation; he is my defence; I shall not be greatly moved.

Psalm 62:1,2

AM I A GOD AT HAND, saith the Lord, and not a God afar off?

Jeremiah 23:23

JESUS ANSWERED and said unto him, If a man love me, he will keep my words: and my Father will love him, and we will come unto him, and make our abode with him.

He that loveth me not keepeth not my sayings: and the word which ye hear is not mine, but the Father's which sent me.

These things have I spoken unto you, being yet present with you.

But the Comforter, which is the Holy Ghost, whom the Father will send in my name, he shall teach you all things, and bring all things to your remembrance, whatsoever I have said unto you.

John 14:23-26

BLESSED BE THE LORD, who daily loadeth us with benefits, even the God of our salvation. Selah.

Psalm 68:19

THEN ONE OF THEM, which was a lawyer, asked him a question, tempting him, and saying,

Master, which is the great commandment in the law?

Jesus said unto him, Thou shalt love the Lord thy God with all thy heart, and with all thy soul, and with all thy mind.

This is the first and great commandment.

And the second is like unto it, Thou shalt love thy neighbour as thyself.

On these two commandments hang all the law and the prophets.

Matthew 22:35-40

SEEK YE THE LORD while he may be found, call ye upon him while he is near:

Let the wicked forsake his way, and the unrighteous man his thoughts: and let him return unto the Lord, and he will have mercy upon him; and to our God, for he will abundantly pardon.

For my thoughts are not your thoughts, neither are your ways my ways, saith the Lord.

For as the heavens are higher than the earth, so are my ways higher than your ways, and my thoughts than your thoughts.

For as the rain cometh down, and the snow from heaven, and returneth not thither, but watereth the earth, and maketh it bring forth and bud, that it may give seed to the sower, and bread to the eater:

So shall my word be that goeth forth out of my mouth: it shall not return unto me void, but it shall accomplish that which I please, and it shall prosper in the thing whereto I sent it.

Isaiah 55:6-11

THY RIGHTEOUSNESS also, O God, is very high, who hast done great things: O God, who is like unto thee!

Thou, which hast shewed me great and sore troubles, shalt quicken me again, and shalt bring me up again from the depths of the earth.

Thou shalt increase my greatness, and comfort me on every side.

Psalm 71:19-21

AND THE LORD went before them by day in a pillar of a cloud, to lead them the way; and by night in a pillar of fire, to give them light; to go by day and night.

Exodus 13:21

FOR THE LORD THY GOD hath blessed thee in all the works of thy hand: he knoweth thy walking through this great wilderness: these forty years the Lord thy God hath been with thee; thou hast lacked nothing.

Deuteronomy 2:7

THEN THEY CRIED unto the Lord in their trouble, and he delivered them out of their distresses.

And he led them forth by the right way, that they might go to a city of habitation.

Oh that men would praise the Lord for his goodness, and for his wonderful works to the children of men!

For he satisfieth the longing soul, and filleth the hungry soul with goodness.

Psalm 107:6-9

FOR THE LORD your God dried up the waters of Jordan from before you, until ye were passed over, as the Lord your God did to the Red sea, which he dried up from before us, until we were gone over:

That all the people of the earth might know the hand of the Lord, that it is mighty: that ye might fear the Lord your God for ever.

Joshua 4:23,24

AND GOD is able to make all grace abound toward you; that ye, always having all sufficiency in all things, may abound to every good work.

II Corinthians 9:8

WHAT TIME I AM AFRAID, I will trust in thee.

In God I will praise his word, in God I have put my trust; I will not fear what flesh can do unto me.

Psalm 56:3,4

THEN WAS THE KING exceeding glad for him, and commanded that they should take Daniel up out of the den. So Daniel was taken up out of the den, and no manner of hurt was found upon him, because he believed in his God.

Daniel 6:23

BUT HE WAS WOUNDED for our transgressions, he was bruised for our iniquities: the chastisement of our peace was upon him; and with his stripes we are healed.

All we like sheep have gone astray; we have turned every one to his own way; and the Lord hath laid on him the iniquity of us all.

Isaiah 53:5,6

BLESS THE LORD, O my soul: and all that is within me, bless his holy name.

Bless the Lord, O my soul, and forget not all his benefits:

Who forgiveth all thine iniquities; who healeth all thy diseases;

Who redeemeth thy life from destruction; who crowneth thee with lovingkindness and tender mercies;

Who satisfieth thy mouth with good things; so that thy youth is renewed like the eagle's.

The Lord executeth righteousness and judgment for all that are oppressed.

Psalm 103:1-6

AND THE SPIRIT OF GOD came upon Azariah the son of Oded:

And he went out to meet Asa, and said unto him, Hear ye me, Asa, and all Judah and Benjamin; The Lord is with you, while ye be with him; and if ye seek him, he will be found of you; but if ye forsake him, he will forsake you.

II Chronicles 15:1,2

AND THE WORLD passeth away, and the lust thereof: but he that doeth the will of God abideth for ever.

I John 2:17

THE STEPS of a good man are ordered by the Lord: and he delighteth in his way.

Though he fall, he shall not be utterly cast down: for the Lord upholdeth him with his hand.

I have been young, and now am old; yet have I not seen the righteous forsaken, nor his seed begging bread.

Psalm 37:23-25

CAST NOT AWAY therefore your confidence, which hath great recompense of reward.

For ye have need of patience, that, after ye have done the will of God, ye might receive the promise.

Hebrews 10:35,36

AND IT shall come to pass, if thou shalt hearken diligently unto the voice of the Lord thy God, to observe and to do all his commandments which I command thee this day, that the Lord thy God will set thee on high above all nations of the earth:

And all these blessings shall come on thee, and overtake thee, if thou shalt hearken unto the voice of the Lord thy God.

Blessed shalt thou be in the city, and blessed shalt thou be in the field.

Blessed shall be the fruit of thy body, and the fruit of thy ground, and the fruit of thy cattle, the increase of thy kine, and the flocks of thy sheep.

Blessed shall be thy basket and thy store.

Blessed shalt thou be when thou comest in, and blessed shalt thou be when thou goest out.

The Lord shall cause thine enemies that rise up against thee to be smitten before thy face: they shall come out against thee one way, and flee before thee seven ways.

The Lord shall command the blessing upon thee in thy storehouses, and in all that thou settest thine hand unto; and he shall bless thee in the land which the Lord thy God giveth thee.

The Lord shall establish thee an holy people unto himself, as he hath sworn unto thee, if thou shalt keep the commandments of the Lord they God, and walk in his ways.

And all people of the earth shall see that thou art called by the name of the Lord; and they shall be afraid of thee.

And the Lord shall make thee plenteous in goods, in the fruit of thy body, and in the fruit of thy cattle, and in the fruit of thy ground, in the land which the Lord sware unto thy fathers to give thee.

The Lord shall open unto thee his good treasure, the heaven to give the rain unto thy land in his season, and to bless all the work of thine hand: and thou shalt lend unto many nations, and thou shalt not borrow.

And the Lord shall make thee the head, and not the tail; and thou shalt be above only, and thou shalt not be beneath; if that thou hearken unto the commandments of the Lord thy God, which I command thee this day, to observe and to do them.

Deuteronomy 28:1-13

MARVELLOUS THINGS did he in the sight of their fathers, in the land of Egypt, in the field of Zoan.

He divided the sea, and caused them to pass through; and he made the waters to stand as an heap.

In the daytime also he led them with a cloud, and all the night with a light of fire.

He clave the rocks in the wilderness, and gave them drink as out of the great depths.

He brought streams also out of the rock, and caused waters to run down like rivers.

Psalm 78:12-16

BE NOT DECEIVED; God is not mocked: for whatsoever a man soweth, that shall he also reap.

For he that soweth to his flesh shall of the flesh reap corruption; but he that soweth to the Spirit shall of the Spirit reap life everlasting.

And let us not be weary in well doing: for in due season we shall reap, if we faint not.

As we have therefore opportunity, let us do good unto all men, especially unto them who are of the household of faith.

Galatians 6:7-10

NOW WE KNOW that God heareth not sinners: but if any man be a worshipper of God, and doeth his will, him he heareth.

John 9:31

CAST THY BURDEN upon the Lord, and he shall sustain thee: he shall never suffer the righteous to be moved.

Psalm 55:22

LIFT UP YOUR EYES to the heavens, and look upon the earth beneath: for the heavens shall vanish away like smoke, and the earth shall wax old like a garment, and they that dwell therein shall die in like manner: but my salvation shall be for ever, and my righteousness shall not be abolished.

Hearken unto me, ye that know righteousness, the people in whose heart is my law; fear ye not the reproach of men, neither be ye afraid of their revilings.

For the moth shall eat them up like a garment, and the worm shall eat them like wool: but my righteousness shall be for ever, and my salvation from generation to generation.

Isaiah 51:6-8

BUT NOW in Christ Jesus ye who sometimes were far off are made nigh by the blood of Christ.

Ephesians 2:13

SHEW ME THY WAYS, O Lord; teach me thy paths.

Lead me in thy truth, and teach me: for thou art the God of my salvation; on thee do I wait all the day.

Remember, O Lord, thy tender mercies and thy lovingkindnesses; for they have been ever of old.

Psalm 25:4-6

FOR AS MANY as are led by the Spirit of God, they are the sons of God.

For ye have not received the spirit of bondage again to fear; but ye have received the Spirit of adoption, whereby we cry, Abba, Father.

The Spirit itself beareth witness with our spirit, that we are the children of God:

And if children, then heirs; heirs of God, and joint-heirs with Christ; if so be that we suffer with him, that we may be also glorified together.

For I reckon that the sufferings of this present time are not worthy to be compared with the glory which shall be revealed in us.

Romans 8:14-18

WHOSOEVER therefore shall confess me before men, him will I confess also before my Father which is in heaven.

But whosoever shall deny me before men, him will I also deny before my Father which is in heaven.

Matthew 10:32,33

IN GOD is my salvation and my glory: the rock of my strength, and my refuge, is in God.

Trust in him at all times; ye people, pour out your heart before him: God is a refuge for us. Selah.

Psalm 62:7,8

FOR I KNOW the thoughts that I think toward you, saith the Lord, thoughts of peace, and not of evil, to give you an expected end.

Then shall ye call upon me, and ye shall go and pray unto me, and I will hearken unto you.

And ye shall seek me, and find me, when ye shall search for me with all your heart.

Jeremiah 29:11-13

FOR THOUGH we walk in the flesh, we do not war after the flesh:

(For the weapons of our warfare are not carnal, but mighty through God to the pulling down of strong holds;)

Casting down imaginations, and every high thing that exalteth itself against the knowledge of God, and bringing into captivity every thought to the obedience of Christ.

II Corinthians 10:3-5

I KNOW that the Lord will maintain the cause of the afflicted, and the right of the poor.

Surely the righteous shall give thanks unto thy name: the upright shall dwell in thy presence.

Psalm 140:12,13

FOR OUR CONVERSATION is in heaven; from whence also we look for the Saviour, the Lord Jesus Christ:

Who shall change our vile body, that it may be fashioned like unto his glorious body, according to the working whereby he is able even to subdue all things unto himself.

Philippians 3:20,21

HAST THOU NOT KNOWN? hast thou not heard, that the everlasting God, the Lord, the Creator of the ends of the earth, fainteth not, neither is weary? there is no searching of his understanding.

He giveth power to the faint; and to them that have no might he increaseth strength.

Even the youths shall faint and be weary, and the young men shall utterly fall:

But they that wait upon the Lord shall renew their strength; they shall mount up with wings as eagles; they shall run, and not be weary; and they shall walk, and not faint.

Isaiah 40:28-31

NOT UNTO US, O LORD, not unto us, but unto thy name give glory, for thy mercy, and for thy truth's sake.

Wherefore should the heathen say, Where is now their God?

But our God is in the heavens: he hath done whatsoever he hath pleased.

Their idols are silver and gold, the work of men's hands.

They have mouths, but they speak not: eyes have they, but they see not:

They have ears, but they hear not: noses have they, but they smell not:

They have hands, but they handle not: feet have they, but they walk not: neither speak they through their throat.

They that make them are like unto them; so is every one that trusteth in them.

O Israel, trust thou in the Lord: he is their help and their shield.

O house of Aaron, trust in the Lord: he is their help and their shield.

Ye that fear the Lord, trust in the Lord: he is their help and their shield.

The Lord hath been mindful of us: he will bless us; he will bless the house of Israel; he will bless the house of Aaron.

He will bless them that fear the Lord, both small and great.

The Lord shall increase you more and more, you and your children.

Ye are blessed of the Lord which made heaven and earth.

The heaven, even the heavens, are the Lord's: but the earth hath he given to the children of men.

The dead praise not the Lord, neither any that go down into silence.

But we will bless the Lord from this time forth and for evermore. Praise the Lord.

Psalm 115

SAY NOT THOU, What is the cause that the former days were better than these? for thou dost not inquire wisely concerning this.

Ecclesiastes 7:10

TO HIM that overcometh will I grant to sit with me in my throne, even as I also overcame, and am set down with my Father in his throne.

Revelation 3:21

THE CHARIOTS OF GOD are twenty thousand, even thousands of angels: the Lord is among them, as in Sinai, in the holy place.

Psalm 68:17

AND HIS NAME through faith in his name hath made this man strong, whom ye see and know: yea, the faith which is by him hath given him this perfect soundness in the presence of you all.

Acts 3:16

FOR THE PROMISE, that he should be the heir of the world, was not to Abraham, or to his seed, through the law, but through the righteousness of faith.

For if they which are of the law be heirs, faith is made void, and the promise made of none effect:

Because the law worketh wrath: for where no law is, there is no transgression.

Therefore it is of faith, that it might be by grace; to the end the promise might be sure to all the seed; not to that only which is of the law, but to that also which is of the faith of Abraham; who is the father of us all.

Romans 4:13-16

BUT if any man love God, the same is known of him.

I Corinthians 8:3

HEAVEN AND EARTH shall pass away: but my words shall not pass away.

Luke 21:33

THY WORD is a lamp unto my feet, and a light unto my path.

Psalm 119:105

MAKE A JOYFUL NOISE unto the Lord, all ye lands.

Serve the Lord with gladness: come before his presence with singing.

Know ye that the Lord he is God: it is he that hath made us, and not we ourselves; we are his people, and the sheep of his pasture.

Enter into his gates with thanksgiving, and into his courts with praise: be thankful unto him, and bless his name.

For the Lord is good; his mercy is everlasting; and his truth endureth to all generations.

Psalm 100

WHEN CHRIST, who is our life, shall appear, then shall ye also appear with him in glory.

Colossians 3:4

LORD, how long wilt thou look on? rescue my soul from their destructions, my darling from the lions.

I will give thee thanks in the great congregation: I will praise thee among much people.

Let not them that are mine enemies wrongfully rejoice over me: neither let them wink with the eye that hate me without a cause.

Psalm 35:17-19

HE THAT HATH my commandments, and keepeth them, he it is that loveth me: and he that loveth me shall be loved of my Father, and I will love him, and will manifest myself to him.

John 14:21

FOR BOTH HE that sanctifieth and they who are sanctified are all of one: for which cause he is not ashamed to call them brethren,

Saying, I will declare thy name unto my brethren, in the midst of the church will I sing praise unto thee.

And again, I will put my trust in him. And again, Behold I and the children which God hath given me.

Forasmuch then as the children are partakers of flesh and blood, he also himself likewise took part of the same; that through death he might destroy him that had the power of death, that is, the devil;

And deliver them who through fear of death were all their lifetime subject to bondage.

For verily he took not on him the nature of angels; but he took on him the seed of Abraham.

Wherefore in all things it behoved him to be made like unto his brethren, that he might be a merciful and faithful high priest in things pertaining to God, to make reconciliation for the sins of the people.

For in that he himself hath suffered being tempted, he is able to succour them that are tempted.

Hebrews 2:11-18

WHEN ISRAEL went out of Egypt, the house of Jacob from a people of strange language;

Judah was his sanctuary, and Israel his dominion.

The sea saw it, and fled: Jordan was driven back.

The mountains skipped like rams, and the little hills like lambs.

What ailed thee, O thou sea, that thou fleddest? thou Jordan, that thou wast driven back?

Ye mountains, that ye skipped like rams; and ye little hills, like lambs?

Tremble, thou earth, at the presence of the Lord, at the presence of the God of Jacob;

Which turned the rock into a standing water, the flint into a fountain of waters.

Psalm 114

YET if any man suffer as a Christian, let him not be ashamed; but let him glorify God on this behalf.

I Peter 4:16

AND MOSES SAID unto the Lord, O my Lord, I am not eloquent, neither heretofore, nor since thou hast spoken unto thy servant: but I am slow of speech, and of a slow tongue.

And the Lord said unto him, Who hath made man's mouth? or who maketh the dumb, or deaf, or the seeing, or the blind? have not I the Lord?

Now therefore go, and I will be with thy mouth, and teach thee what thou shalt say.

Exodus 4:10-12

O FEAR THE LORD, ye his saints: for there is no want to them that fear him.

The young lions do lack, and suffer hunger: but they that seek the Lord shall not want any good thing.

Psalm 34:9,10

THEN SPAKE JOSHUA to the Lord in the day when the Lord delivered up the Amorites before the children of Israel, and he said in the sight of Israel, Sun, stand thou still upon Gibeon; and thou, Moon, in the valley of Ajalon.

And the sun stood still, and the moon stayed, until the people had avenged themselves upon their enemies. Is not this written in the book of Jasher? So the sun stood still in the midst of heaven, and hasted not to go down about a whole day.

And there was no day like that before it or after it, that the Lord hearkened unto the voice of a man: for the Lord fought for Israel.

Joshua 10:12-14

AND I COMMANDED Joshua at that time, saying, Thine eyes have seen all that the Lord your God hath done unto these two kings: so shall the Lord do unto all the kingdoms whither thou passest.

Ye shall not fear them: for the Lord your God he shall fight for you.

Deuteronomy 3:21,22

NEVERTHELESS he regarded their affliction, when he heard their cry:

And he remembered for them his covenant, and repented according to the multitude of his mercies.

Psalm 106:44,45

IN WHAT PLACE therefore ye hear the sound of the trumpet, resort ye thither unto us: our God shall fight for us.

Nehemiah 4:20

AND I WILL PRAY the Father, and he shall give you another Comforter, that he may abide with you for ever;

Even the Spirit of truth; whom the world cannot receive, because it seeth him not, neither knoweth him: but ye know him; for he dwelleth with you, and shall be in you.

I will not leave you comfortless: I will come to you.

John 14:16-18

GOD HATH SPOKEN once; twice have I heard this; that power belongeth unto God.

Also unto thee, O Lord, belongeth mercy: for thou renderest to every man according to his work.

Psalm 62:11,12

AND I WILL betroth thee unto me for ever; yea, I will betroth thee unto me in righteousness, and in judgment, and in lovingkindness, and in mercies.

I will even betroth thee unto me in faithfulness: and thou shalt know the Lord.

And it shall come to pass in that day, I will hear, saith the Lord, I will hear the heavens, and they shall hear the earth;

And the earth shall hear the corn, and the wine, and the oil; and they shall hear Jezreel.

And I will sow her unto me in the earth; and I will have mercy upon her that had not obtained mercy; and I will say to them which were not my people, Thou art my people; and they shall say, Thou art my God.

Hosea 2:19-23

REJOICE IN THE LORD alway: and again I say, Rejoice.

Philippians 4:4

O LORD, thou hast searched me, and known me.

Thou knowest my downsitting and mine uprising, thou understandest my thought afar off.

Thou compassest my path and my lying down, and art acquainted with all my ways.

For there is not a word in my tongue, but, lo, O Lord, thou knowest it altogether.

Thou hast beset me behind and before, and laid thine hand upon me.

Such knowledge is too wonderful for me; it is high, I cannot attain unto it.

Whither shall I go from thy spirit? or whither shall I flee from thy presence?

If I ascend up into heaven, thou art there: if I make my bed in hell, behold, thou art there.

If I take the wings of the morning, and dwell in the uttermost parts of the sea;

Even there shall thy hand lead me, and thy right hand shall hold me.

If I say, Surely the darkness shall cover me; even the night shall be light about me.

Yea, the darkness hideth not from thee; but the night shineth as the day: the darkness and the light are both alike to thee.

For thou hast possessed my reins: thou hast covered me in my mother's womb.

I will praise thee; for I am fearfully and wonderfully made: marvellous are thy works; and that my soul knoweth right well.

My substance was not hid from thee, when I was made in secret, and curiously wrought in the lowest parts of the earth.

Thine eyes did see my substance, yet being unperfect; and in thy book all my members were written, which in continuance were fashioned, when as yet there was none of them.

How precious also are thy thoughts unto me, O God! how great is the sum of them!

If I should count them, they are more in number than the sand: when I awake, I am still with thee.

Surely thou wilt slay the wicked, O God: depart from me therefore, ye bloody men.

For they speak against thee wickedly, and thine enemies take thy name in vain.

Do not I hate them, O Lord, that hate thee? and am not I grieved with those that rise up against thee?

I hate them with perfect hatred: I count them mine enemies.

Search me, O God, and know my heart: try me, and know my thoughts:

And see if there be any wicked way in me, and lead me in the way everlasting.

Psalm 139

AND THEY that be wise shall shine as the brightness of the firmament; and they that turn many to righteousness as the stars for ever and ever.

Daniel 12:3

TWO ARE BETTER than one; because they have a good reward for their labour.

For if they fall, the one will lift up his fellow: but woe to him that is alone when he falleth; for he hath not another to help him up.

Ecclesiastes 4:9,10

O GOD, when thou wentest forth before thy people, when thou didst march through the wilderness; Selah:

The earth shook, the heavens also dropped at the presence of God: even Sinai itself was moved at the presence of God, the God of Israel.

Thou, O God, didst send a plentiful rain, whereby thou didst confirm thine inheritance, when it was weary.

Psalm 68:7-9

HO, EVERY ONE that thirsteth, come ye to the waters, and he that hath no money; come ye, buy, and eat; yea, come, buy wine and milk without money and without price.

Wherefore do ye spend money for that which is not bread? and your labour for that which satisfieth not? hearken diligently unto me, and eat ye that which is good, and let your soul delight itself in fatness.

Incline your ear, and come unto me: hear, and your soul shall live; and I will make an everlasting covenant with you, even the sure mercies of David.

Isaiah 55:1-3

AND I SAY UNTO YOU my friends, Be not afraid of them that kill the body, and after that have no more that they can do.

But I will forewarn you whom ye shall fear: Fear him, which after he hath killed hath power to cast into hell; yea, I say unto you, Fear him.

Luke 12:4,5

BUT THOU art he that took me out of the womb: thou didst make me hope when I was upon my mother's breasts.

I was cast upon thee from the womb: thou art my God from my mother's belly.

Psalm 22:9,10

BEHOLD, what manner of love the Father hath bestowed upon us, that we should be called the sons of God: therefore the world knoweth us not, because it knew him not.

Beloved, now are we the sons of God, and it doth not yet appear what we shall be: but we know that, when he shall appear, we shall be like him; for we shall see him as he is.

I John 3:1,2

BUT WITHOUT FAITH it is impossible to please him: for he that cometh to God must believe that he is, and that he is a rewarder of them that diligently seek him.

Hebrews 11:6

BUT THE SALVATION of the righteous is of the Lord: he is their strength in the time of trouble.

And the Lord shall help them, and deliver them: he shall deliver them from the wicked, and save them, because they trust in him.

Psalm 37:39,40

BUT GOD BE THANKED, that ye were the servants of sin, but ye have obeyed from the heart that form of doctrine which was delivered you.

Being then made free from sin, ye became the servants of righteousness.

Romans 6:17,18

THE LORD by wisdom hath founded the earth; by understanding hath he established the heavens.

By his knowledge the depths are broken up, and the clouds drop down the dew.

My son, let not them depart from thine eyes: keep sound wisdom and discretion:

So shall they be life unto thy soul, and grace to thy neck.

Then shalt thou walk in thy way safely, and thy foot shall not stumble.

When thou liest down, thou shalt not be afraid: yea, thou shalt lie down, and thy sleep shall be sweet.

Be not afraid of sudden fear, neither of the desolation of the wicked, when it cometh.

For the Lord shall be thy confidence, and shall keep thy foot from being taken.

Withhold not good from them to whom it is due, when it is in the power of thine hand to do it.

Proverbs 3:19-27

FROM THE RISING of the sun unto the going down of the same the Lord's name is to be praised.

The Lord is high above all nations, and his glory above the heavens.

Who is like unto the Lord our God, who dwelleth on high,

Who humbleth himself to behold the things that are in heaven, and in the earth!

He raiseth up the poor out of the dust, and lifteth the needy out of the dunghill;

That he may set him with princes, even with the princes of his people.

He maketh the barren woman to keep house, and to be a joyful mother of children. Praise ye the Lord.

Psalm 113:3-9

AND I HEARD a loud voice saying in heaven, Now is come salvation, and strength, and the kingdom of our God, and the power of his Christ: for the accuser of our brethren is cast down, which accused them before our God day and night.

And they overcame him by the blood of the Lamb, and by the word of their testimony; and they loved not their lives unto the death.

Revelation 12:10,11

THERE HATH no temptation taken you but such as is common to man: but God is faithful, who will not suffer you to be tempted above that ye are able; but will with the temptation also make a way to escape, that ye may be able to bear it.

I Corinthians 10:13

AS FOR ME, I will call upon God; and the Lord shall save me.

Evening, and morning, and at noon, will I pray, and cry aloud: and he shall hear my voice.

Psalm 55:16,17

BEHOLD, I AM THE LORD, the God of all flesh: is there any thing too hard for me?

Jeremiah 32:27

BUT I WOULD not have you to be ignorant, brethren, concerning them which are asleep, that ye sorrow not, even as others which have no hope.

For if we believe that Jesus died and rose again, even so them also which sleep in Jesus will God bring with him.

For this we say unto you by the word of the Lord that we which are alive and remain unto the coming of the Lord shall not prevent them which are asleep.

For the Lord himself shall descend from heaven with a shout, with the voice of the archangel, and with the trump of God: and the dead in Christ shall rise first:

Then we which are alive and remain shall be caught up together with them in the clouds, to meet the Lord in the air: and so shall we ever be with the Lord.

Wherefore comfort one another with these words.

I Thessalonians 4:13-18

WE HAVE HEARD with our ears, O God, our fathers have told us, what work thou didst in their days, in the times of old.

How thou didst drive out the heathen with thy hand, and plantedst them; how thou didst afflict the people, and cast them out.

For they got not the land in possession by their own sword, neither did their own arm save them: but thy right hand, and thine arm, and the light of thy countenance, because thou hadst a favour unto them.

Psalm 44:1-3

BUT THE LORD was with Joseph, and shewed him mercy, and gave him favour in the sight of the keeper of the prison.

Genesis 39:21

FEAR THOU NOT; for I am with thee: be not dismayed; for I am thy God: I will strengthen thee; yea, I will help thee; yea, I will uphold thee with the right hand of my righteousness.

Behold, all they that were incensed against thee shall be ashamed and confounded: they shall be as nothing; and they that strive with thee shall perish.

Thou shalt seek them, and shalt not find them, even them that contended with thee: they that war against thee shall be as nothing, and as a thing of nought.

For I the Lord thy GOD will hold thy right hand, saying unto thee, Fear not; I will help thee.

Isaiah 41:10-13

I SAID UNTO THE LORD, Thou art my God: hear the voice of my supplications, O Lord.

O God the Lord, the strength of my salvation thou hast covered my head in the day of battle.

Psalm 140:6,7

MY SHEEP hear my voice, and I know them, and they follow me:

And I give unto them eternal life; and they shall never perish, neither shall any man pluck them out of my hand.

My Father, which gave them me, is greater than all; and no man is able to pluck them out of my Father's hand.

John 10:27-29

IS ANY AMONG YOU afflicted? let him pray. Is any merry? let him sing psalms.

Is any sick among you? let him call for the elders of the church; and let them pray over him, anointing him with oil in the name of the Lord:

And the prayer of faith shall save the sick, and the Lord shall raise him up; and if he have committed sins, they shall be forgiven him.

James 5:13-15

THY MERCY, O LORD, is in the heavens; and thy faithfulness reacheth unto the clouds.

Thy righteousness is like the great mountains; thy judgments are a great deep: O Lord, thou preservest man and beast.

How excellent is thy lovingkindness, O God! therefore the children of men put their trust under the shadow of thy wings.

Psalm 36:5-7

BUT YE that did cleave unto the Lord your God are alive every one of you this day.

Deuteronomy 4:4

STAND FAST therefore in the liberty wherewith Christ hath made us free, and be not entangled again with the yoke of bondage.

Galatians 5:1

FOR WHO IS GOD save the Lord? or who is a rock save our God?

It is God that girdeth me with strength, and maketh my way perfect.

He maketh my feet like hinds' feet, and setteth me upon my high places.

He teacheth my hands to war, so that a bow of steel is broken by mine arms.

Thou hast also given me the shield of thy salvation: and thy right hand hath holden me up, and thy gentleness hath made me great.

Thou hast enlarged my steps under me, that my feet did not slip.

I have pursued mine enemies, and overtaken them: neither did I turn again till they were consumed.

I have wounded them that they were not able to rise: they are fallen under my feet.

For thou hast girded me with strength unto the battle: thou has subdued under me those that rose up against me.

Thou hast also given me the necks of mine enemies; that I might destroy them that hate me.

Psalm 18:31-40

BUT GODLINESS with contentment is great gain.

For we brought nothing into this world, and it is certain we can carry nothing out.

And having food and raiment let us be therewith content.

I Timothy 6:6-8

AND HE SAID, Whereunto shall we liken the kingdom of God? or with what comparison shall we compare it?

It is like a grain of mustard seed, which, when it is sown in the earth, is less than all the seeds that be in the earth:

But when it is sown, it groweth up, and becometh greater than all herbs, and shooteth out great branches; so that the fowls of the air may lodge under the shadow of it.

Mark 4:30-32

FOR EVER, O LORD, thy word is settled in heaven.

Thy faithfulness is unto all generations: thou hast established the earth, and it abideth.

Psalm 119:89,90

FOR THROUGH HIM we both have access by one Spirit unto the Father.

Now therefore ye are no more strangers and foreigners, but fellowcitizens with the saints, and of the household of God;

And are built upon the foundation of the apostles and prophets, Jesus Christ himself being the chief corner stone;

In whom all the building fitly framed together groweth unto an holy temple in the Lord:

In whom ye also are builded together for an habitation of God through the Spirit.

Ephesians 2:18-22

HUMBLE YOURSELVES therefore under the mighty hand of God, that he may exalt you in due time:

Casting all your care upon him; for he careth for you.

I Peter 5:6,7

THROUGH THEE will we push down our enemies: through thy name will we tread them under that rise up against us.

For I will not trust in my bow, neither shall my sword save me.

But thou hast saved us from our enemies, and hast put them to shame that hated us.

In God we boast all the day long, and praise thy name for ever. Selah.

Psalm 44:5-8

AND ALL these kings and their land did Joshua take at one time, because the Lord God of Israel fought for Israel.

Joshua 10:42

THEN UPON JAHAZIEL the son of Zechariah, the son of Benaiah, the son of Jeiel, the son of Mattaniah, a levite of the sons of Asaph, came the spirit of the Lord in the midst of the congregation;

And he said, Hearken ye, all Judah, and ye inhabitants of Jerusalem, and thou king Jehoshaphat, Thus saith the Lord unto you, Be not afraid nor dismayed by reason of this great multitude; for the battle is not yours, but God's.

To morrow go ye down against them: behold, they come up by the cliff of Ziz; and ye shall find them at the end of the brook, before the wilderness of Jeruel.

Ye shall not need to fight in this battle: set yourselves, stand ye still, and see the salvation of the Lord with you, O Judah and Jerusalem: fear not, nor be dismayed; to morrow go out against them: for the Lord will be with you.

II Chronicles 20:14-17

I AM THE LORD THY GOD, which brought thee out of the land of Egypt: open thy mouth wide, and I will fill it.

Psalm 81:10

THEN HE SAID unto them, Go your way, eat the fat, and drink the sweet, and send portions unto them for whom nothing is prepared: for this day is holy unto our Lord: neither be ye sorry; for the joy of the Lord is your strength.

Nehemiah 8:10

AND WHATSOEVER ye shall ask in my name, that will I do, that the Father may be glorified in the Son.

If ye shall ask any thing in my name, I will do it.

If ye love me, keep my commandments.
John 14:13-15

WHY ART THOU cast down, O my soul? and why art thou disquieted within me? hope in God: for I shall yet praise him, who is the health of my countenance, and my God.

Psalm 43:5

FOR GOD hath not appointed us to wrath, but to obtain salvation by our Lord Jesus Christ,

Who died for us, that, whether we wake or sleep, we should live together with him.

Wherefore comfort yourselves together, and edify one another, even as also ye do.
I Thessalonians 5:9-11

IF YE WALK in my statutes, and keep my commandments, and do them;

Then I will give you rain in due season, and the land shall yield her increase, and the trees of the field shall yield their fruit.

And your threshing shall reach unto the vintage, and the vintage shall reach unto the sowing time: and ye shall eat your bread to the full, and dwell in your land safely.

And I will give peace in the land, and ye shall lie down, and none shall make you afraid: and I will rid evil beasts out of the land, neither shall the sword go through your land.

And ye shall chase your enemies, and they shall fall before you by the sword.

And five of you shall chase an hundred, and an hundred of you shall put ten thousand to flight: and your enemies shall fall before you by the sword.

For I will have respect unto you, and make you fruitful, and multiply you, and establish my covenant with you.

And ye shall eat old store, and bring forth the old because of the new.

And I will set my tabernacle among you: and my soul shall not abhor you.

And I will walk among you, and will be your God, and ye shall be my people.

Leviticus 26:3-12

BUT THE MERCY of the Lord is from everlasting to everlasting upon them that fear him, and his righteousness unto children's children;

To such as keep his covenant, and to those that remember his commandments to do them.

The Lord hath prepared his throne in the heavens; and his kingdom ruleth over all.

Psalm 103:17-19

AND GOD SAID unto him, Because thou hast asked this thing, and hast not asked for thyself long life; neither hast asked riches for thyself, nor hast asked the life of thine enemies; but hast asked for thyself understanding to discern judgment;

Behold, I have done according to thy words: lo, I have given thee a wise and an understanding heart; so that there was none like thee before thee, neither after thee shall any arise like unto thee.

And I have also given thee that which thou hast not asked, both riches, and honour: so that there shall not be any among the kings like unto thee all thy days.

And if thou wilt walk in my ways, to keep my statutes and my commandments, as thy father David did walk, then I will lengthen thy days.

I Kings 3:11-14

AND ISAAC entreated the Lord for his wife, because she was barren: and the Lord was entreated of him, and Rebekah his wife conceived.

Genesis 25:21

LORD, how are they increased that trouble me! many are they that rise up against me.

Many there be which say of my soul, There is no help for him in God. Selah.

But thou, O Lord, art a shield for me; my glory, and the lifter up of mine head.

I cried unto the Lord with my voice, and he heard me out of his holy hill. Selah.

Psalm 3:1-4

AND THOUGH THE LORD give you the bread of adversity, and the water of affliction, yet shall not thy teachers be removed into a corner any more, but thine eyes shall see thy teachers:

And thine ears shall hear a word behind thee, saying, This is the way, walk ye in it, when ye turn to the right hand, and when ye turn to the left.

Isaiah 30:20,21

ARE NOT five sparrows sold for two farthings, and not one of them is forgotten before God?

But even the very hairs of your head are all numbered. Fear not therefore: ye are of more value than many sparrows.

Luke 12:6,7

I WILL PRAISE THEE with my whole heart: before the gods will I sing praise unto thee.

I will worship toward thy holy temple, and praise thy name for thy lovingkindness and for thy truth: for thou hast magnified thy word above all thy name.

In the day when I cried thou answeredst me, and strengthenedst me with strength in my soul.

Psalm 138:1-3

BE CAREFUL for nothing; but in every thing by prayer and supplication with thanksgiving let your requests be made known unto God.

And the peace of God, which passeth all understanding, shall keep your hearts and minds through Christ Jesus.

Philippians 4:6,7

FIGHT THE GOOD FIGHT of faith, lay hold on eternal life, whereunto thou art also called, and hast professed a good profession before many witnesses.

I Timothy 6:12

WITH THE MERCIFUL thou wilt shew thyself merciful; with an upright man thou wilt shew thyself upright;

With the pure thou wilt shew thyself pure; and with the froward thou wilt shew thyself froward.

For thou wilt save the afflicted people; but wilt bring down high looks.

For thou wilt light my candle: the Lord my God will enlighten my darkness.

For by thee I have run through a troop; and by my God have I leaped over a wall.

As for God, his way is perfect: the word of the Lord is tried: he is a buckler to all those that trust in him.

Psalm 18:25-30

WHEREFORE seeing we also are compassed about with so great a cloud of witnesses, let us lay aside every weight, and the sin which doth so easily beset us, and let us run with patience the race that is set before us,

Looking unto Jesus the author and finisher of our faith; who for the joy that was set before him endured the cross, despising the shame, and is set down at the right hand of the throne of God.

Hebrews 12:1,2

BUT UNTO every one of us is given grace according to the measure of the gift of Christ.

Ephesians 4:7

LET THE PEOPLE praise thee, O God; let all the people praise thee.

Then shall the earth yield her increase; and God, even our own God, shall bless us.

God shall bless us; and all the ends of the earth shall fear him.

Psalm 67:5-7

JESUS SAID UNTO HIM, If thou canst believe, all things are possible to him that believeth.

Mark 9:23

WHEN THE POOR AND NEEDY seek water, and there is none, and their tongue faileth for thirst, I the Lord will hear them, I the God of Israel will not forsake them.

I will open rivers in high places, and fountains in the midst of the valleys: I will make the wilderness a pool of water, and the dry land springs of water.

I will plant in the wilderness the cedar, the shittah tree, and the myrtle, and the oil tree; I will set in the desert the fir tree, and the pine, and the box tree together:

That they may see, and know, and consider, and understand together, that the hand of the Lord hath done this, and the Holy One of Israel hath created it.

Isaiah 41:17-20

O GIVE THANKS unto the Lord; for he is good: for his mercy endureth for ever.

O give thanks unto the God of gods: for his mercy endureth for ever.

O give thanks to the Lord of lords: for his mercy endureth for ever.

To him who alone doeth great wonders: for his mercy endureth for ever.

To him that by wisdom made the heavens: for his mercy endureth for ever.

To him that stretched out the earth above the waters: for his mercy endureth for ever.

To him that made great lights: for his mercy endureth for ever:

The sun to rule by day: for his mercy endureth for ever:

The moon and stars to rule by night: for his mercy endureth for ever.

To him that smote Egypt in their first-born: for his mercy endureth for ever:

And brought out Israel from among them: for his mercy endureth for ever:

With a strong hand, and with a stretched out arm: for his mercy endureth for ever.

To him which divided the Red sea into parts: for his mercy endureth for ever:

And made Israel to pass through the midst of it: for his mercy endureth for ever:

But overthrew Pharaoh and his host in the Red sea: for his mercy endureth for ever.

To him which led his people through the wilderness: for his mercy endureth for ever.

To him which smote great kings: for his mercy endureth for ever:

And slew famous kings: for his mercy endureth for ever:

Sihon king of the Amorites: for his mercy endureth for ever:

And Og the king of Bashan: for his mercy endureth for ever:

And gave their land for an heritage: for his mercy endureth for ever:

Even an heritage unto Israel his servant: for his mercy endureth for ever.

Who remembered us in our low estate: for his mercy endureth for ever:

And hath redeemed us from our enemies: for his mercy endureth for ever.

Who giveth food to all flesh: for his mercy endureth for ever.

O give thanks unto the God of heaven: for his mercy endureth for ever.

Psalm 136

SUBMIT YOURSELVES therefore to God. Resist the devil, and he will flee from you.

Draw nigh to God, and he will draw nigh to you. Cleanse your hands, ye sinners; and purify your hearts, ye double minded.

James 4:7,8

YE ARE OF GOD, little children, and have overcome them: because greater is he that is in you, than he that is in the world.

I John 4:4

IN THE DAY of my trouble I will call upon thee: for thou wilt answer me.

Psalm 86:7

THE CUP OF BLESSING which we bless, is it not the communion of the blood of Christ? The bread which we break, is it not the communion of the body of Christ?

For we being many are one bread, and one body: for we are all partakers of that one bread.

I Corinthians 10:16,17

GREAT PEACE have they which love thy law: and nothing shall offend them.
Psalm 119:165

THY HANDS have made me and fashioned me: give me understanding, that I may learn thy commandments.

They that fear thee will be glad when they see me; because I have hoped in thy word.

I know, O Lord, that thy judgments are right, and that thou in faithfulness hast afflicted me.

Let, I pray thee, thy merciful kindness be for my comfort, according to thy word unto thy servant.

Let thy tender mercies come unto me, that I may live: for thy law is my delight.
Psalm 119:73-77

BUT IF from thence thou shalt seek the Lord thy God, thou shalt find him, if thou seek him with all thy heart and with all thy soul.
Deuteronomy 4:29

GRACE AND PEACE be multiplied unto you through the knowledge of God, and of Jesus our Lord,

According as his divine power hath given unto us all things that pertain unto life and godliness, through the knowledge of him that hath called us to glory and virtue:

Whereby are given unto us exceeding great and precious promises: that by these ye might be partakers of the divine nature, having escaped the corruption that is in the world through lust.

II Peter 1:2-4

BLESSED IS THE MAN that walketh not in the counsel of the ungodly, nor standeth in the way of sinners, nor sitteth in the seat of the scornful.

But his delight is in the law of the Lord; and in his law doth he meditate day and night.

And he shall be like a tree planted by the rivers of water, that bringeth forth his fruit in his season; his leaf also shall not wither; and whatsoever he doeth shall prosper.

Psalm 1:1-3

BUT YE ARE NOT in the flesh, but in the Spirit, if so be that the Spirit of God dwell in you. Now if any man have not the Spirit of Christ, he is none of his.

And if Christ be in you, the body is dead because of sin; but the Spirit is life because of righteousness.

But if the Spirit of him that raised up Jesus from the dead dwell in you, he that raised up Christ from the dead shall also quicken your mortal bodies by his Spirit that dwelleth in you.

Romans 8:9-11

BUT WHEN the fulness of the time was come, God sent forth his Son, made of a woman, made under the law,

To redeem them that were under the law, that we might receive the adoption of sons.

And because ye are sons, God hath sent forth the Spirit of his Son into your hearts, crying, Abba, Father.

Wherefore thou art no more a servant, but a son; and if a son, then an heir of God through Christ.

Galatians 4:4-7

O GOD, thou art my God; early will I seek thee: my soul thirsteth for thee, my flesh longeth for thee in a dry and thirsty land, where no water is;

To see thy power and thy glory, so as I have seen thee in the sanctuary.

Because thy lovingkindness is better than life, my lips shall praise thee.

Thus will I bless thee while I live: I will lift up my hands in thy name.

My soul shall be satisfied as with marrow and fatness; and my mouth shall praise thee with joyful lips:

When I remember thee upon my bed, and meditate on thee in the night watches.

Because thou hast been my help, therefore in the shadow of thy wings will I rejoice.

My soul followeth hard after thee: thy right hand upholdeth me.

Psalm 63:1-8

THERE FAILED NOT ought of any good thing which the Lord had spoken unto the house of Israel; all came to pass.

Joshua 21:45

AND JESUS SAID UNTO THEM, I am the bread of life: he that cometh to me shall never hunger; and he that believeth on me shall never thirst.

But I said unto you, That ye also have seen me, and believe not.

All that the Father giveth me shall come to me; and him that cometh to me I will in no wise cast out.

For I came down from heaven, not to do mine own will, but the will of him that sent me.

And this is the Father's will which hath sent me, that of all which he hath given me I should lose nothing, but should raise it up again at the last day.

And this is the will of him that sent me, that every one which seeth the Son, and believeth on him, may have everlasting life: and I will raise him up at the last day.

John 6:35-40

THE SACRIFICES OF GOD are a broken spirit: a broken and a contrite heart, O God, thou wilt not despise.

Psalm 51:17

THEN JOB AROSE, and rent his mantle, and shaved his head, and fell down upon the ground, and worshipped,

And said, Naked came I out of my mother's womb, and naked shall I return thither: the Lord gave, and the Lord hath taken away; blessed be the name of the Lord.

In all this Job sinned not, nor charged God foolishly.

Job 1:20-22

AND I SAW a new heaven and a new earth: for the first heaven and the first earth were passed away; and there was no more sea.

And I John saw the holy city, new Jerusalem, coming down from God out of heaven, prepared as a bride adorned for her husband.

And I heard a great voice out of heaven saying, Behold, the tabernacle of God is with men, and he will dwell with them, and they shall be his people, and God himself shall be with them, and be their God.

And God shall wipe away all tears from their eyes; and there shall be no more death, neither sorrow, nor crying, neither shall there be any more pain: for the former things are passed away.

Revelation 21:1-4

THROUGH GOD we shall do valiantly: for he it is that shall tread down our enemies.

Psalm 108:13

BEHOLD, the Lord's hand is not shortened, that it cannot save; neither his ear heavy, that it cannot hear.

Isaiah 59:1

WHEREFORE I put thee in remembrance that thou stir up the gift of God, which is in thee by the putting on of my hands.

For God hath not given us the spirit of fear; but of power, and of love, and of a sound mind.

II Timothy 1:6,7

THE LORD is merciful and gracious, slow to anger, and plenteous in mercy.

He will not always chide: neither will he keep his anger for ever.

He hath not dealt with us after our sins; nor rewarded us according to our iniquities.

For as the heaven is high above the earth, so great is his mercy toward them that fear him.

As far as the east is from the west, so far hath he removed our transgressions from us.

Like as a father pitieth his children, so the Lord pitieth them that fear him.

Psalm 103:8-13

THEREFORE ALSO NOW, saith the Lord, turn ye even to me with all your heart, and with fasting, and with weeping, and with mourning:

And rend your heart, and not your garments, and turn unto the Lord your God: for he is gracious and merciful, slow to anger, and of great kindness, and repenteth him of the evil.

Joel 2:12,13

BUT THE FRUIT of the Spirit is love, joy, peace, longsuffering, gentleness, goodness, faith,

Meekness, temperance: against such there is no law.

And they that are Christ's have crucified the flesh with the affections and lusts.

If we live in the Spirit, let us also walk in the Spirit.

Galatians 5:22-25

BUT KNOW that the Lord hath set apart him that is godly for himself: the Lord will hear when I call unto him.

Psalm 4:3

THEREFORE I will look unto the Lord; I will wait for the God of my salvation: my God will hear me.

Rejoice not against me, O mine enemy: when I fall, I shall arise; when I sit in darkness, the Lord shall be a light unto me.

Micah 7:7,8

I KNOW that, whatsoever God doeth, it shall be for ever: nothing can be put to it, nor any thing taken from it: and God doeth it, that men should fear before him.

Ecclesiastes 3:14

IT IS GOOD FOR ME that I have been afflicted; that I might learn thy statutes.

The law of thy mouth is better unto me than thousands of gold and silver.

Psalm 119:71,72

HITHERTO have ye asked nothing in my name: ask, and ye shall receive, that your joy may be full.

These things have I spoken unto you in proverbs: but the time cometh, when I shall no more speak unto you in proverbs, but I shall shew you plainly of the Father.

At that day ye shall ask in my name: and I say not unto you, that I will pray the Father for you:

For the Father himself loveth you, because ye have loved me, and have believed that I came out from God.

John 16:24-27

COME UNTO ME, all ye that labour and are heavy laden, and I will give you rest.

Take my yoke upon you, and learn of me; for I am meek and lowly in heart: and ye shall find rest unto your souls.

For my yoke is easy, and my burden is light.

Matthew 11:28-30

THEN THEY that feared the Lord spake often one to another: and the Lord hearkened, and heard it, and a book of remembrance was written before him for them that feared the Lord, and that thought upon his name.

And they shall be mine, saith the Lord of hosts, in that day when I make up my jewels; and I will spare them, as a man spareth his own son that serveth him.

Malachi 3:16,17

BLESS THE LORD, O my soul. O Lord my God, thou art very great; thou art clothed with honour and majesty.

Who coverest thyself with light as with a garment: who stretchest out the heavens like a curtain:

Who layeth the beams of his chambers in the waters: who maketh the clouds his chariot: who walketh upon the wings of the wind:

Who maketh his angels spirits; his ministers a flaming fire:

Who laid the foundations of the earth, that it should not be removed for ever.

Thou coveredst it with the deep as with a garment: the waters stood above the mountains.

At thy rebuke they fled; at the voice of thy thunder they hasted away.

They go up by the mountains; they go down by the valleys unto the place which thou hast founded for them.

Thou hast set a bound that they may not pass over; that they turn not again to cover the earth.

He sendeth the springs into the valleys, which run among the hills.

They give drink to every beast of the field: the wild asses quench their thirst.

By them shall the fowls of the heaven have their habitation, which sing among the branches

He watereth the hills from his chambers: the earth is satisfied with the fruit of thy works.

He causeth the grass to grow for the cattle, and herb for the service of man: that he may bring forth food out of the earth;

And wine that maketh glad the heart of man, and oil to make his face to shine, and bread which strengtheneth man's heart.

The trees of the Lord are full of sap; the cedars of Lebanon, which he hath planted;

Where the birds make their nests: as for the stork, the fir trees are her house.

The high hills are a refuge for the wild goats; and the rocks for the conies.

He appointed the moon for seasons: the sun knoweth his going down.

Thou makest darkness, and it is night: wherein all the beasts of the forest do creep forth.

The young lions roar after their prey, and seek their meat from God.

The sun ariseth, they gather themselves together, and lay them down in their dens.

Man goeth forth unto his work and to his labour until the evening.

O Lord, how manifold are thy works! in wisdom hast thou made them all: the earth is full of thy riches.

So is this great and wide sea, wherein are things creeping innumerable, both small and great beasts.

There go the ships: there is that leviathan, whom thou hast made to play therein.

These wait all upon thee; that thou mayest give them their meat in due season.

That thou givest them they gather: thou openest thine hand, they are filled with good.

Thou hidest thy face, they are troubled: thou takest away their breath, they die, and return to their dust.

Thou sendest forth thy spirit, they are created: and thou renewest the face of the earth.

The glory of the Lord shall endure for ever: the Lord shall rejoice in his works.

He looketh on the earth, and it trembleth: he toucheth the hills, and they smoke.

I will sing unto the Lord as long as I live: I will sing praise to my God while I have my being.

My meditation of him shall be sweet: I will be glad in the Lord.

Let the sinners be consumed out of the earth, and let the wicked be no more. Bless thou the Lord, O my soul. Praise ye the Lord.

Psalm 104

AND HE BELIEVED in the Lord; and he counted it to him for righteousness.

Genesis 15:6

BEHOLD, I shew you a mystery; We shall not all sleep, but we shall all be changed,

In a moment, in the twinkling of an eye, at the last trump: for the trumpet shall sound, and the dead shall be raised incorruptible, and we shall be changed.

For this corruptible must put on incorruption, and this mortal must put on immortality.

So when this corruptible shall have put on incorruption, and this mortal shall have put on immortality, then shall be brought to pass the saying that is written, Death is swallowed up in victory.

O death, where is thy sting? O grave, where is thy victory?

I Corinthians 15:51-55

THEY THAT SOW in tears shall reap in joy.

He that goeth forth and weepeth, bearing precious seed, shall doubtless come again with rejoicing, bringing his sheaves with him.

Psalm 126:5,6

SING, O HEAVENS; and be joyful, O earth; and break forth into singing, O mountains: for the Lord hath comforted his people, and will have mercy upon his afflicted.

Isaiah 49:13

EVERY GOOD GIFT and every perfect gift is from above, and cometh down from the Father of lights, with whom is no variableness, neither shadow of turning.

Of his own will begat he us with the word of truth, that we should be a kind of firstfruits of his creatures.

James 1:17,18

WHEN MINE ENEMIES are turned back, they shall fall and perish at thy presence.

For thou hast maintained my right and my cause; thou satest in the throne judging right.

Psalm 9:3,4

FINALLY, BRETHREN, whatsoever things are true, whatsoever things are honest, whatsoever things are just, whatsoever things are pure, whatsoever things are lovely, whatsoever things are of good report; if there be any virtue, and if there be any praise, think on these things.

Philippians 4:8

REMEMBER YE NOT the former things, neither consider the things of old.

Behold, I will do a new thing; now it shall spring forth; shall ye not know it? I will even make a way in the wilderness, and rivers in the desert.

Isaiah 43:18,19

BUT VERILY God hath heard me; he hath attended to the voice of my prayer.

Blessed be God, which hath not turned away my prayer, nor his mercy from me.

Psalm 66:19,20

FOR WHATSOEVER is born of God overcometh the world: and this is the victory that overcometh the world, even our faith.

Who is he that overcometh the world, but he that believeth that Jesus is the Son of God?

I John 5:4,5

THIS IS A FAITHFUL SAYING, and worthy of all acceptation, that Christ Jesus came into the world to save sinners; of whom I am chief.

I Timothy 1:15

NOW KNOW I that the Lord saveth his anointed; he will hear him from his holy heaven with the saving strength of his right hand.

Psalm 20:6

AND THOU SHALT remember all the way which the Lord thy God led thee these forty years in the wilderness, to humble thee, and to prove thee, to know what was in thine heart, whether thou wouldest keep his commandments, or no.

And he humbled thee, and suffered thee to hunger, and fed thee with manna, which thou knewest not, neither did thy fathers know; that he might make thee know that man doth not live by bread only, but by every word that proceedeth out of the mouth of the Lord doth man live.

Thy raiment waxed not old upon thee, neither did thy foot swell, these forty years.

Thou shalt also consider in thine heart, that, as a man chasteneth his son, so the Lord thy God chasteneth thee.

Therefore thou shalt keep the commandments of the Lord thy God, to walk in his ways, and to fear him.

For the Lord thy God bringeth thee into a good land, a land of brooks of water, of fountains and depths that spring out of valleys and hills;

A land of wheat, and barley, and vines, and fig trees, and pomegranates; a land of oil olive, and honey;

A land wherein thou shalt eat bread without scarceness, thou shalt not lack any thing in it; a land whose stones are iron, and out of whose hills thou mayest dig brass.

When thou hast eaten and art full, then thou shalt bless the Lord thy God for the good land which he hath given thee.

Deuteronomy 8:2-10

THE SPIRIT OF THE LORD is upon me, because he hath anointed me to preach the gospel to the poor; he hath sent me to heal the brokenhearted, to preach deliverance to the captives, and recovering of sight to the blind, to set at liberty them that are bruised,

To preach the acceptable year of the Lord.

And he closed the book, and he gave it again to the minister, and sat down. And the eyes of all them that were in the synagogue were fastened on him.

And he began to say unto them, This day is this scripture fulfilled in your ears.

Luke 4:18-21

YET THE LORD will command his lovingkindness in the daytime, and in the night his song shall be with me, and my prayer unto the God of my life.

Psalm 42:8

FOR WHOM the Lord loveth he chasteneth, and scourgeth every son whom he receiveth.

If ye endure chastening, God dealeth with you as with sons; for what son is he whom the father chasteneth not?

But if ye be without chastisement, whereof all are partakers, then are ye bastards, and not sons.

Furthermore we have had fathers of our flesh which corrected us, and we gave them reverence: shall we not much rather be in subjection unto the Father of spirits, and live?

For they verily for a few days chastened us after their own pleasure; but he for our profit, that we might be partakers of his holiness.

Now no chastening for the present seemeth to be joyous, but grievous: nevertheless afterward it yieldeth the peaceable fruit of righteousness unto them which are exercised thereby.

Hebrews 12:6-11

THE LORD is not slack concerning his promise, as some men count slackness; but is longsuffering to us-ward, not willing that any should perish, but that all should come to repentance.

II Peter 3:9

THEN THEY CRY unto the Lord in their trouble, and he saveth them out of their distresses.

He sent his word, and healed them, and delivered them from their destructions.

Oh that men would praise the Lord for his goodness, and for his wonderful works to the children of men!

And let them sacrifice the sacrifices of thanksgiving, and declare his works with rejoicing.

Psalm 107:19-22

KNOW THEREFORE that the Lord thy God, he is God, the faithful God, which keepeth covenant and mercy with them that love him and keep his commandments to a thousand generations.

Deuteronomy 7:9

AND BE YE KIND one to another, tenderhearted, forgiving one another, even as God for Christ's sake hath forgiven you.

Ephesians 4:32

THOU VISITEST the earth, and waterest it: thou greatly enrichest it with the river of God, which is full of water: thou preparest them corn, when thou hast so provided for it.

Thou waterest the ridges thereof abundantly: thou settlest the furrows thereof: thou makest it soft with showers: thou blessest the springing thereof.

Thou crownest the year with thy goodness; and thy paths drop fatness.

They drop upon the pastures of the wilderness: and the little hills rejoice on every side.

The pastures are clothed with flocks; the valleys also are covered over with corn; they shout for joy, they also sing.

Psalm 65:9-13

WHAT SHALL WE THEN SAY to these things? If God be for us, who can be against us?

He that spared not his own Son, but delivered him up for us all, how shall he not with him also freely give us all things?

Romans 8:31,32

THOMAS SAITH UNTO HIM, Lord, we know not whither thou goest; and how can we know the way?

Jesus saith unto him, I am the way, the truth, and the life: no man cometh unto the Father, but by me.

If ye had known me, ye should have known my Father also: and from henceforth ye know him, and have seen him.

Philip saith unto him, Lord, shew us the Father, and it sufficeth us.

Jesus saith unto him, Have I been so long time with you, and yet hast thou not known me, Philip? he that hath seen me hath seen the Father; and how sayest thou then, Shew us the Father?

Believest thou not that I am in the Father, and the Father in me? the words that I speak unto you I speak not of myself: but the Father that dwelleth in me, he doeth the works.

Believe me that I am in the Father, and the Father in me: or else believe me for the very works' sake.

Verily, verily, I say unto you, He that believeth on me, the works that I do shall he do also; and greater works than these shall he do; because I go unto my Father.

John 14:5-12

AND THEY that know thy name will put their trust in thee: for thou, Lord, hast not forsaken them that seek thee.

Psalm 9:10

AND YE HAVE SEEN all that the Lord your God hath done unto all these nations because of you; for the Lord your God is he that hath fought for you.

Joshua 23:3

THE LORD LIVETH; and blessed be my rock; and exalted be the God of the rock of my salvation.

It is God that avengeth me, and that bringeth down the people under me,

And that bringeth me forth from mine enemies: thou also hast lifted me up on high above them that rose up against me: thou hast delivered me from the violent man.

Therefore I will give thanks unto thee, O Lord, among the heathen, and I will sing praises unto thy name.

He is the tower of salvation for his king: and sheweth mercy to his anointed, unto David, and to his seed for evermore.

II Samuel 22:47-51

BLESSED IS THE MAN whom thou chastenest, O Lord, and teachest him out of thy law;

That thou mayest give him rest from the days of adversity, until the pit be digged for the wicked.

For the Lord will not cast off his people, neither will he forsake his inheritance.

But judgment shall return unto righteousness: and all the upright in heart shall follow it.

Who will rise up for me against the evildoers? or who will stand up for me against the workers of iniquity?

Unless the Lord had been my help, my soul had almost dwelt in silence.

When I said, My foot slippeth; thy mercy, O Lord, held me up.

In the multitude of my thoughts within me thy comforts delight my soul.

Psalm 94:12-19

BLESSED ARE THEY that do his commandments, that they may have right to the tree of life, and may enter in through the gates into the city.

Revelation 22:14

AND HE SAID unto me, My grace is sufficient for thee: for my strength is made perfect in weakness. Most gladly therefore will I rather glory in my infirmities, that the power of Christ may rest upon me.

Therefore I take pleasure in infirmities, in reproaches, in necessities, in persecutions, in distresses for Christ's sake: for when I am weak, then am I strong.

II Corinthians 12:9,10

HENCEFORTH there is laid up for me a crown of righteousness, which the Lord, the righteous judge, shall give me at that day: and not to me only, but unto all them also that love his appearing.

II Timothy 4:8

AND IT SHALL BE, that thou shalt drink of the brook; and I have commanded the ravens to feed thee there.

I Kings 17:4

WHOSO OFFERETH PRAISE
glorifieth me: and to him that ordereth his conversation aright will I shew the salvation of God.
Psalm 50:23

YET MAN IS BORN unto trouble, as the
sparks fly upward.

I would seek unto God, and unto God
would I commit my cause:

Which doeth great things and unsearchable;
marvellous things without number.
Job 5:7-9

BE NOT AFRAID, ye beasts of the field:
for the pastures of the wilderness do spring, for
the tree beareth her fruit, the fig tree and the vine
do yield their strength.

Be glad then, ye children of Zion, and
rejoice in the Lord your God: for he hath given
you the former rain moderately, and he will
cause to come down for you the rain, the former
rain, and the latter rain in the first month.

And the floors shall be full of wheat, and
the vats shall overflow with wine and oil.

And I will restore to you the years that
the locust hath eaten, the cankerworm, and the
caterpillar, and the palmerworm, my great army
which I sent among you.

And ye shall eat in plenty, and be satisfied, and praise the name of the Lord your God, that hath dealt wondrously with you: and my people shall never be ashamed.

And ye shall know that I am in the midst of Israel, and that I am the Lord your God, and none else: and my people shall never be ashamed.

Joel 2:22-27

O BLESS OUR GOD, ye people, and make the voice of his praise to be heard:

Which holdeth our soul in life, and suffereth not our feet to be moved.

For thou, O God, hast proved us: thou has tried us, as silver is tried.

Thou broughtest us into the net; thou laidst affliction upon our loins.

Thou hast caused men to ride over our heads; we went through fire and through water: but thou broughtest us out into a wealthy place.

Psalm 66:8-12

. . . AND THE LORD preserved David whithersoever he went.

II Samuel 8:6b

THESE THINGS I have spoken unto you, that in me ye might have peace. In the world ye shall have tribulation: but be of good cheer; I have overcome the world.

John 16:33

THE LORD KNOWETH the days of the upright: and their inheritance shall be for ever.

They shall not be ashamed in the evil time: and in the days of famine they shall be satisfied.

Psalm 37:18,19

GRACE BE TO YOU and peace from God the Father, and from our Lord Jesus Christ,

Who gave himself for our sins, that he might deliver us from this present evil world, according to the will of God and our Father:

To whom be glory for ever and ever. Amen.

Galatians 1:3-5

BETTER IS THE END of a thing than the beginning thereof: and the patient in spirit is better than the proud in spirit.

Ecclesiastes 7:8

THEY THAT TRUST in the Lord shall be as mount Zion, which cannot be removed, but abideth for ever.

As the mountains are round about Jerusalem, so the Lord is round about his people from henceforth even for ever.

Psalm 125:1,2

THE LORD IS GOOD, a strong hold in the day of trouble; and he knoweth them that trust in him.

Nahum 1:7

FOR WHOSOEVER shall do the will of my Father which is in heaven, the same is my brother, and sister, and mother.

Matthew 12:50

THEN THOU SPAKEST in vision to thy holy one, and saidst, I have laid help upon one that is mighty; I have exalted one chosen out of the people.

I have found David my servant; with my holy oil have I anointed him:

With whom my hand shall be established: mine arm also shall strengthen him.

The enemy shall not exact upon him; nor the son of wickedness afflict him.

And I will beat down his foes before his face, and plague them that hate him.

But my faithfulness and my mercy shall be with him: and in my name shall his horn be exalted.

I will set his hand also in the sea, and his right hand in the rivers.

He shall cry unto me, Thou art my father, my God, and the rock of my salvation.

Also I will make him my firstborn, higher than the kings of the earth.

My mercy will I keep for him for evermore, and my covenant shall stand fast with him.

His seed also will I make to endure for ever, and his throne as the days of heaven.

If his children forsake my law, and walk not in my judgments;

If they break my statutes, and keep not my commandments;

Then will I visit their transgression with the rod, and their iniquity with stripes.

Nevertheless my lovingkindness will I not utterly take from him, nor suffer my faithfulness to fail.

My covenant will I not break, nor alter the thing that is gone out of my lips.

Once have I sworn by my holiness that I will not lie unto David.

His seed shall endure for ever, and his throne as the sun before me.

It shall be established for ever as the moon, and as a faithful witness in heaven. Selah.

Psalm 89:19-37

I WILL GREATLY REJOICE in the Lord, my soul shall be joyful in my God; for he hath clothed me with the garments of salvation, he hath covered me with the robe of righteousness, as a bridegroom decketh himself with ornaments, and as a bride adorneth herself with her jewels.

For as the earth bringeth forth her bud, and as the garden causeth the things that are sown in it to spring forth; so the Lord GOD will cause righteousness and praise to spring forth before all the nations.

Isaiah 61:10,11

BLESSED IS THE MAN that endureth temptation: for when he is tried, he shall receive the crown of life, which the Lord hath promised to them that love him.

James 1:12

THE MIGHTY GOD, even the Lord, hath spoken, and called the earth from the rising of the sun unto the going down thereof.

Out of Zion, the perfection of beauty, God hath shined.

Psalm 50:1,2

BLESSED BE GOD, even the Father of our Lord Jesus Christ, the Father of mercies, and the God of all comfort;

Who comforteth us in all our tribulation, that we may be able to comfort them which are in any trouble, by the comfort wherewith we ourselves are comforted of God.

For as the sufferings of Christ abound in us, so our consolation also aboundeth by Christ.

And whether we be afflicted, it is for your consolation and salvation, which is effectual in the enduring of the same sufferings which we also suffer: or whether we be comforted, it is for your consolation and salvation.

II Corinthians 1:3-6

HE STAGGERED not at the promise of God through unbelief; but was strong in faith, giving glory to God;

And being fully persuaded that, what he had promised, he was able also to perform.

Romans 4:20,21

OH HOW GREAT is thy goodness, which thou hast laid up for them that fear thee; which thou hast wrought for them that trust in thee before the sons of men!

Thou shalt hide them in the secret of thy presence from the pride of man: thou shalt keep them secretly in a pavilion from the strife of tongues.

Psalm 31:19,20

AND IT SHALL come to pass, if ye shall hearken diligently unto my commandments which I command you this day, to love the Lord your God, and to serve him with all your heart and with all your soul,

That I will give you the rain of your land in his due season, the first rain and the latter rain, that thou mayest gather in thy corn, and thy wine, and thine oil.

And I will send grass in thy fields for thy cattle, that thou mayest eat and be full.

Deuteronomy 11:13-15

BLESSED BE the God and Father of our Lord Jesus Christ, who hath blessed us with all spiritual blessings in heavenly places in Christ:

According as he hath chosen us in him before the foundation of the world, that we should be holy and without blame before him in love:

Having predestinated us unto the adoption of children by Jesus Christ to himself, according to the good pleasure of his will,

To the praise of the glory of his grace, wherein he hath made us accepted in the beloved.

In whom we have redemption through his blood, the forgiveness of sins, according to the riches of his grace;

Wherein he hath abounded toward us in all wisdom and prudence;

Having made known unto us the mystery of his will, according to his good pleasure which he hath purposed in himself:

That in the dispensation of the fulness of times he might gather together in one all things in Christ, both which are in heaven, and which are on earth; even in him:

In whom also we have obtained an inheritance, being predestinated according to the purpose of him who worketh all things after the counsel of his own will:

That we should be to the praise of his glory, who first trusted in Christ.

In whom ye also trusted, after that ye heard the word of truth, the gospel of your salvation: in whom also after that ye believed, ye were sealed with that holy Spirit of promise,

Which is the earnest of our inheritance until the redemption of the purchased possession, unto the praise of his glory.

Ephesians 1:3-14

THE RIGHTEOUS shall flourish like the palm tree: he shall grow like a cedar in Lebanon.

Those that be planted in the house of the Lord shall flourish in the courts of our God.

They shall still bring forth fruit in old age; they shall be fat and flourishing;

To shew that the Lord is upright: he is my rock, and there is no unrighteousness in him.

Psalm 92:12-15

AND JESUS ANSWERING said unto them, They that are whole need not a physician; but they that are sick.

I came not to call the righteous, but sinners to repentance.

Luke 5:31,32

I, EVEN I, am he that blotteth out thy transgressions for mine own sake, and will not remember thy sins.

Isaiah 43:25

FOR THE OPPRESSION of the poor, for the sighing of the needy, now will I arise, saith the Lord; I will set him in safety from him that puffeth at him.

The words of the Lord are pure words: as silver tried in a furnace of earth, purified seven times.

Psalm 12:5,6

AND NOAH BUILDED an altar unto the Lord; and took of every clean beast, and of every clean fowl, and offered burnt offerings on the altar.

And the Lord smelled a sweet savour; and the Lord said in his heart, I will not again curse the ground any more for man's sake; for the imagination of man's heart is evil from his youth; neither will I again smite any more every thing living, as I have done.

While the earth remaineth, seedtime and harvest, and cold and heat, and summer and winter, and day and night shall not cease.

Genesis 8:20-22

LET YOUR CONVERSATION be without covetousness; and be content with such things as ye have: for he hath said, I will never leave thee, nor forsake thee.

So that we may boldly say, The Lord is my helper, and I will not fear what man shall do unto me.

Hebrews 13:5,6

I WAITED PATIENTLY for the Lord; and he inclined unto me, and heard my cry.

He brought me up also out of an horrible pit, out of the miry clay, and set my feet upon a rock, and established my goings.

And he hath put a new song in my mouth, even praise unto our God: many shall see it, and fear, and shall trust in the Lord.

Psalm 40:1-3

BEHOLD, happy is the man whom God correcteth: therefore despise not thou the chastening of the Almighty.

Job 5:17

IN HOPE OF eternal life, which God, that cannot lie, promised before the world began.

Titus 1:2

HAVE MERCY upon me, O Lord; for I am weak: O Lord, heal me; for my bones are vexed.

My soul is also sore vexed: but thou, O Lord, how long?

Return, O Lord, deliver my soul: oh save me for thy mercies' sake.

For in death there is no remembrance of thee: in the grave who shall give thee thanks?

I am weary with my groaning; all the night make I my bed to swim; I water my couch with my tears.

Mine eye is consumed because of grief; it waxeth old because of all mine enemies.

Depart from me, all ye workers of iniquity; for the Lord hath heard the voice of my weeping.

The Lord hath heard my supplication; the Lord will receive my prayer.

Psalm 6:2-9

NOT THAT I SPEAK in respect of want: for I have learned, in whatsoever state I am, therewith to be content.

I know both how to be abased, and I know how to abound: every where and in all things I am instructed both to be full and to be hungry, both to abound and to suffer need.

I can do all things through Christ which strengtheneth me.

Philippians 4:11-13

JESUS SAID UNTO HER, I am the resurrection, and the life: he that believeth in me, though he were dead, yet shall he live:

And whosoever liveth and believeth in me shall never die. Believest thou this?

John 11:25,26

O SING UNTO THE LORD a new song; for he hath done marvellous things: his right hand, and his holy arm, hath gotten him the victory.

The Lord hath made known his salvation: his righteousness hath he openly shewed in the sight of the heathen.

He hath remembered his mercy and his truth toward the house of Israel: all the ends of the earth have seen the salvation of our God.

Make a joyful noise unto the Lord, all the earth: make a loud noise, and rejoice, and sing praise.

Sing unto the Lord with the harp; with the harp, and the voice of a psalm.

With trumpets and sound of cornets make a joyful noise before the Lord, the King.

Let the sea roar, and the fulness thereof; the world, and they that dwell therein.

Let the floods clap their hands: let the hills be joyful together

Before the Lord; for he cometh to judge the earth: with righteousness shall he judge the world, and the people with equity.

Psalm 98

ONE MAN OF YOU shall chase a thousand: for the Lord your God, he it is that fighteth for you, as he hath promised you.

Joshua 23:10

AND THE LORD said unto Gideon, The people that are with thee are too many for me to give the Midianites into their hands, lest Israel vaunt themselves against me, saying, Mine own hand hath saved me.

Judges 7:2

THIS IS THE DAY which the Lord hath made; we will rejoice and be glad in it.

Psalm 118:24

AND IT shall come to pass in that day, that the mountains shall drop down new wine, and the hills shall flow with milk, and all the rivers of Judah shall flow with waters, and a fountain shall come forth of the house of the Lord, and shall water the valley of Shittim.

Egypt shall be a desolation, and Edom shall be a desolate wilderness, for the violence against the children of Judah, because they have shed innocent blood in their land.

But Judah shall dwell for ever, and Jerusalem from generation to generation.

For I will cleanse their blood that I have not cleansed: for the Lord dwelleth in Zion.

Joel 3:18-21

THESE THINGS have I written unto you that believe on the name of the Son of God; that ye may know that ye have eternal life, and that ye may believe on the name of the Son of God.

And this is the confidence that we have in him, that, if we ask any thing according to his will, he heareth us:

And if we know that he hear us, whatsoever we ask, we know that we have the petitions that we desired of him.

If any man see his brother sin a sin which is not unto death, he shall ask, and he shall give him life for them that sin not unto death. There is a sin unto death: I do not say that he shall pray for it.

I John 5:13-16

BE STILL, and know that I am God: I will be exalted among the heathen, I will be exalted in the earth.

The Lord of hosts is with us; the God of Jacob is our refuge. Selah.

Psalm 46:10,11

BLESSED BE THE LORD, that hath given rest unto his people Israel, according to all that he promised: there hath not failed one word of all his good promise, which he promised by the hand of Moses his servant.

I Kings 8:56

THE LORD THY GOD in the midst of thee is mighty; he will save, he will rejoice over thee with joy; he will rest in his love, he will joy over thee with singing.

Zephaniah 3:17

THEN THEY CRIED unto the Lord in their trouble, and he saved them out of their distresses.

He brought them out of darkness and the shadow of death, and brake their bands in sunder.

Oh that men would praise the Lord for his goodness, and for his wonderful works to the children of men!

For he hath broken the gates of brass, and cut the bars of iron in sunder.

Psalm 107:13-16

I WILL STAND upon my watch, and set me upon the tower, and will watch to see what he will say unto me, and what I shall answer when I am reproved.

Habakkuk 2:1

O RIGHTEOUS FATHER, the world hath not known thee: but I have known thee, and these have known that thou hast sent me.

And I have declared unto them thy name, and will declare it: that the love wherewith thou hast loved me may be in them, and I in them.

John 17:25,26

ONE THING have I desired of the Lord, that will I seek after; that I may dwell in the house of the Lord all the days of my life, to behold the beauty of the Lord, and to inquire in his temple.

For in the time of trouble he shall hide me in his pavilion: in the secret of his tabernacle shall he hide me; he shall set me up upon a rock.

Psalm 27:4,5

IN THE DAY of prosperity be joyful, but in the day of adversity consider: God also hath set the one over against the other, to the end that man should find nothing after him.

Ecclesiastes 7:14

EVEN AS ABRAHAM believed God, and it was accounted to him for righteousness.

Know ye therefore that they which are of faith, the same are the children of Abraham.

And the scripture, foreseeing that God would justify the heathen through faith, preached before the gospel unto Abraham, saying, In thee shall all nations be blessed.

So then they which be of faith are blessed with faithful Abraham.

For as many as are of the works of the law are under the curse: for it is written, Cursed is every one that continueth not in all things which are written in the book of the law to do them.

But that no man is justified by the law in the sight of God, it is evident: for, The just shall live by faith.

And the law is not of faith: but, The man that doeth them shall live in them.

Christ hath redeemed us from the curse of the law, being made a curse for us: for it is written, Cursed is every one that hangeth on a tree:

That the blessing of Abraham might come on the Gentiles through Jesus Christ; that we might receive the promise of the Spirit through faith.

Galatians 3:6-14

THE RIGHT HAND of the Lord is exalted: the right hand of the Lord doeth valiantly.

I shall not die, but live, and declare the works of the Lord.

The Lord hath chastened me sore: but he hath not given me over unto death.

Psalm 118:16-18

NOW THANKS be unto God, which always causeth us to triumph in Christ, and maketh manifest the savour of his knowledge by us in every place.

II Corinthians 2:14

FOR THUS SAITH the Lord God of Israel, The barrel of meal shall not waste, neither shall the cruse of oil fail, until the day that the Lord sendeth rain upon the earth.

I Kings 17:14

THE RIGHTEOUS CRY, and the Lord heareth, and delivereth them out of all their troubles.

The Lord is nigh unto them that are of a broken heart; and saveth such as be of a contrite spirit.

Many are the afflictions of the righteous: but the Lord delivereth him out of them all.

Psalm 34:17-19

FOR SINCE THE BEGINNING of the world men have not heard, nor perceived by the ear, neither hath the eye seen, O God, beside thee, what he hath prepared for him that waiteth for him.

Isaiah 64:4

THEREFORE being justified by faith, we have peace with God through our Lord Jesus Christ:

By whom also we have access by faith into this grace wherein we stand, and rejoice in hope of the glory of God.

And not only so, but we glory in tribulations also: knowing that tribulation worketh patience;

And patience, experience; and experience, hope:

And hope maketh not ashamed; because the love of God is shed abroad in our hearts by the Holy Ghost which is given unto us.

For when we were yet without strength, in due time Christ died for the ungodly.

Romans 5:1-6

WE HAVE THOUGHT of thy lovingkindness, O God, in the midst of thy temple.

According to thy name, O God, so is thy praise unto the ends of the earth: thy right hand is full of righteousness.

Let Mount Zion rejoice, let the daughters of Judah be glad, because of thy judgments.

Walk about Zion, and go round about her: tell the towers thereof.

Mark ye well her bulwarks, consider her palaces; that ye may tell it to the generation following.

For this God is our God for ever and ever: he will be our guide even unto death.

Psalm 48:9-14

BUT MY GOD shall supply all your need according to his riches in glory by Christ Jesus.

Philippians 4:19

AGAIN, the kingdom of heaven is like unto treasure hid in a field; the which when a man hath found, he hideth, and for joy thereof goeth and selleth all that he hath, and buyeth that field.

Again, the kingdom of heaven is like unto a merchant man, seeking goodly pearls:

Who, when he had found one pearl of great price, went and sold all that he had, and bought it.

Matthew 13:44-46

WITHHOLD NOT THOU thy tender mercies from me, O Lord: let thy lovingkindness and thy truth continually preserve me.

Psalm 40:11

LET NOT your heart be troubled: ye believe in God, believe also in me.

In my Father's house are many mansions: if it were not so, I would have told you. I go to prepare a place for you.

And if I go and prepare a place for you, I will come again, and receive you unto myself; that where I am, there ye may be also.

And whither I go ye know, and the way ye know.

John 14:1-4

FOR I KNOW that my redeemer liveth, and that he shall stand at the latter day upon the earth:

And though after my skin worms destroy this body, yet in my flesh shall I see God:

Whom I shall see for myself, and mine eyes shall behold, and not another; though my reins be consumed within me.

Job 19:25-27

IF IT HAD NOT BEEN the Lord who was on our side, now may Israel say;

If it had not been the Lord who was on our side, when men rose up against us:

Then they had swallowed us up quick, when their wrath was kindled against us:

Then the waters had overwhelmed us, the stream had gone over our soul:

Then the proud waters had gone over our soul.

Blessed be the Lord, who hath not given us as a prey to their teeth.

Our soul is escaped as a bird out of the snare of the fowlers: the snare is broken, and we are escaped.

Our help is in the name of the Lord, who made heaven and earth.

Psalm 124

AND GOD SAID, Behold, I have given you every herb bearing seed, which is upon the face of all the earth, and every tree, in the which is the fruit of a tree yielding seed; to you it shall be for meat.

And to every beast of the earth, and to every fowl of the air, and to every thing that creepeth upon the earth, wherein there is life, I have given every green herb for meat: and it was so.

Genesis 1:29,30

YET NOW HEAR, O Jacob my servant; and Israel, whom I have chosen:

Thus saith the Lord that made thee, and formed thee from the womb, which will help thee; Fear not, O Jacob, my servant; and thou, Jesurun, whom I have chosen.

For I will pour water upon him that is thirsty, and floods upon the dry ground: I will pour my spirit upon thy seed, and my blessing upon thine offspring:

And they shall spring up as among the grass, as willows by the water courses.

Isaiah 44:1-4

GOD is greatly to be feared in the assembly of the saints, and to be had in reverence of all them that are about him.

O Lord God of hosts, who is a strong Lord like unto thee? or to thy faithfulness round about thee?

Thou rulest the raging of the sea: when the waves thereof arise, thou stillest them.

Thou hast broken Rahab in pieces, as one that is slain; thou hast scattered thine enemies with thy strong arm.

The heavens are thine, the earth also is thine: as for the world and the fulness thereof, thou hast founded them.

The north and the south thou hast created them: Tabor and Hermon shall rejoice in thy name.

Thou hast a mighty arm: strong is thy hand, and high is thy right hand.

Justice and judgment are the habitation of thy throne: mercy and truth shall go before thy face.

Blessed is the people that know the joyful sound: they shall walk, O Lord, in the light of thy countenance.

In thy name shall they rejoice all the day: and in thy righteousness shall they be exalted.

For thou art the glory of their strength: and in thy favour our horn shall be exalted.

For the Lord is our defence; and the Holy One of Israel is our king.

Psalm 89:7-18

GIVE, and it shall be given unto you; good measure, pressed down, and shaken together, and running over, shall men give into your bosom. For with the same measure that ye mete withal it shall be measured to you again.

Luke 6:38

BE STRONG and of a good courage, fear not, nor be afraid of them: for the Lord thy God, he it is that doth go with thee; he will not fail thee, nor forsake thee.

Deuteronomy 31:6

BUT LET ALL THOSE that put their trust in thee rejoice: let them ever shout for joy, because thou defendest them: let them also that love thy name be joyful in thee.

For thou, Lord, wilt bless the righteous; with favour wilt thou compass him as with a shield.

Psalm 5:11,12

MY BRETHREN, count it all joy when ye fall into divers temptations;

Knowing this, that the trying of your faith worketh patience.

But let patience have her perfect work, that ye may be perfect and entire, wanting nothing.

If any of you lack wisdom, let him ask of God, that giveth to all men liberally, and upbraideth not; and it shall be given him.

But let him ask in faith, nothing wavering. For he that wavereth is like a wave of the sea driven with the wind and tossed.

For let not that man think that he shall receive any thing of the Lord.

A double minded man is unstable in all his ways.

James 1:2-8

WHEREFORE the law was our schoolmaster to bring us unto Christ, that we might be justified by faith.

But after that faith is come, we are no longer under a schoolmaster.

For ye are all the children of God by faith in Christ Jesus.

For as many of you as have been baptized into Christ have put on Christ.

There is neither Jew nor Greek, there is neither bond nor free, there is neither male nor female: for ye are all one in Christ Jesus.

And if ye be Christ's, then are ye Abraham's seed, and heirs according to the promise.

Galatians 3:24-29

FOR THOU, LORD, hast made me glad through thy work: I will triumph in the works of thy hands.

Psalm 92:4

FOR WE OURSELVES also were sometimes foolish, disobedient, deceived, serving divers lusts and pleasures, living in malice and envy, hateful, and hating one another.

But after that the kindness and love of God our Saviour toward man appeared,

Not by works of righteousness which we have done, but according to his mercy he saved us, by the washing of regeneration, and renewing of the Holy Ghost;

Which he shed on us abundantly through Jesus Christ our Saviour;

That being justified by his grace, we should be made heirs according to the hope of eternal life.

Titus 3:3-7

AS FOR GOD, his way is perfect; the word of the Lord is tried: he is a buckler to all them that trust in him.

For who is God, save the Lord? and who is a rock, save our God?

God is my strength and power: and he maketh my way perfect.

He maketh my feet like hinds' feet: and setteth me upon my high places.

He teacheth my hands to war; so that a bow of steel is broken by mine arms.

Thou hast also given me the shield of thy salvation: and thy gentleness hath made me great.

Thou hast enlarged my steps under me; so that my feet did not slip.

I have pursued mine enemies, and destroyed them; and turned not again until I had consumed them.

And I have consumed them, and wounded them, that they could not arise: yea, they are fallen under my feet.

For thou hast girded me with strength to battle: them that rose up against me hast thou subdued under me.

Thou hast also given me the necks of mine enemies, that I might destroy them that hate me.

They looked, but there was none to save; even unto the Lord, but he answered them not.

Then did I beat them as small as the dust of the earth, I did stamp them as the mire of the street, and did spread them abroad.

II Samuel 22:31-43

WAIT ON THE LORD: be of good courage, and he shall strengthen thine heart: wait, I say, on the Lord.

Psalm 27:14

AND, BEHOLD, this day I am going the way of all the earth: and ye know in all your hearts and in all your souls, that not one thing hath failed of all the good things which the Lord your God spake concerning you; all are come to pass unto you, and not one thing hath failed thereof.

Joshua 23:14

BUT UNTO YOU that fear my name shall the Sun of righteousness arise with healing in his wings; and ye shall go forth, and grow up as calves of the stall.

Malachi 4:2

THERE IS A RIVER, the streams whereof shall make glad the city of God, the holy place of the tabernacles of the most High.

God is in the midst of her; she shall not be moved: God shall help her, and that right early.

The heathen raged, the kingdoms were moved: he uttered his voice, the earth melted.

The Lord of hosts is with us; the God of Jacob is our refuge. Selah.

Psalm 46:4-7

GOD IS OUR REFUGE and strength, a very present help in trouble.

Therefore will not we fear, though the earth be removed, and though the mountains be carried into the midst of the sea;

Though the waters thereof roar and be troubled, though the mountains shake with the swelling thereof. Selah.

Psalm 46:1-3

NOTES

NOTES

ISBN 1-55748-295-0